COMPLETELY
UP STEPHEN'S BRAE

by

Charles Bannerman

**A final reflection of life at Inverness Royal Academy at
Midmills and Culduthel**

1

COMPLETELY UP STEPHEN'S BRAE

Printed by For The Right Reasons, Grant Street, Inverness.
fortherightreasons@rocketmail.com or 01463 718844

Published by Inverness Royal Academy.

ISBN 978-1-905787-92-0

THE AUTHOR

Charles Bannerman was born in Inverness and was brought up in the Dalneigh area of the town where he spent his entire schooldays. Educated at Dalneigh Primary School and the Royal Academy, he graduated from Edinburgh University with first class honours in Chemistry in 1975.

After a year at Aberdeen College of Education and a further year teaching Maths at Millburn Secondary School, he joined the Chemistry Department at the Royal Academy in 1977, remaining there until his retiral in 2013, which coincides with the publication of this book. He became a Senior Teacher and the school's press officer and newsletter editor in 1995.

For most of his working life he has operated a dual career in teaching and freelance sports journalism. He has been the Inverness Courier's athletics correspondent since 1976 and for the BBC in Inverness covered athletics before becoming local sports reporter in 1984. He also regularly broadcasts nationally, including football coverage for both radio and television, and has been BBC Scotland's shinty correspondent since 2011. He was Highland Sports Reporter of the Year in 2001 and 2005.

In addition to what are now four "Stephen's Brae" books he also wrote "Against All Odds", Inverness Caledonian Thistle's official history of the merger which saw the creation of that club. A Life Member of Inverness Harriers, which he first joined in 1969, he has been involved in athletics as a competitor, coach and committee member and has coached a number of athletes to Commonwealth Games and Great Britain teams in a variety of events. His two grown up children Martin and Jenny are both former pupils of the Royal Academy and both live and work in Inverness.

ACKNOWLEDGEMENTS

It is always difficult to know where to start acknowledgements for a book like this but on this occasion I just have to give pride of place to the many interviewees who supplied me with the anecdotes about school life which appear throughout. Their input was both informative and enlightening and has contributed greatly to the content. One strong common factor also emerged repeatedly throughout these interviews and that was a pride in the institution which is Inverness Royal Academy.

A lengthy interview with former Depute Rector Bill Walker, who also provided some illustrations, revealed a great deal about the Culduthel era in particular. Meanwhile at the other end of the timescale, Angus MacKenzie's recollections began as a pupil during World War II and he also had a particularly good insight into the character of D.J. MacDonald who emerges as the dominant personality of this book.

Other ex-members of staff who had input were Archie Fraser, Patsy Forbes and Leo Longmore while there were pupil memories from Ian Philip, Colin Fettes, Marion Hughes (Renfrew), Tom McCook, Hugh Grant and Katie Gibb (Rennie) who was Midmills' last Head Girl.

As always, these Stephen's Brae books are published by the school with profits to the school fund, and I am grateful to the Rector, Alastair McKinlay, for agreeing to this fourth effort.

Apart from putting together the words and choosing the illustrations, desktop publishing is essential and the input and expertise of Carole Matheson has been vital in that area.

Big thanks also to the Rev Richard Burkitt and Kevin Swanson at For The Right Reasons who have made such a good job of the printing and brilliantly guided me technically through the final stages of production.

Inverness College have also been extremely helpful in granting access to the Midmills building and permission to publish the photographs taken during that visit.

The illustrations include excerpts from school magazines and photographs from the school archive which Robert Preece has conscientiously kept for many years now. Thanks also to Shona MacKinnon, Head Teacher of Dalneigh Primary School, for access to the photo of the school football team in Chapter 1 and also to my old Dalneigh and Royal Academy schoolmate Roddy Williamson for the class photo in the same chapter.

One difficulty with writing acknowledgements before a book is published is that there are bound to be others whose assistance only becomes apparent at a later date. With previous books this has especially been the case with sales and distribution, so these so far unidentified individuals I thank in anticipation.

HISTORICAL NOTE

Here I am going to try to summarsie a long and distinguished history in a single page! Almost 800 years ago in 1233 a Monastic School was founded in Inverness by a group of Black Friars near where Friars Street currently is. By the mid 1500s this had evolved into one of the Grammar Schools which were beginning to appear. That relocated to Bank Lane in 1574 and then to Dunbar's Hospital in Church Street in 1688. Here a Major James Wolfe, who was on the Duke of Cumberland's staff at Culloden, took mathematics lessons. In 1759 and now a General, he led the British army which captured Quebec during the Seven Years War, but with fatal consequences for himself.

The Grammar School metamorphosed into Inverness Academy which was opened in 1792 in a new building on New Street, now Academy Street. July 16th, 1792 is therefore the official foundation date of the school. Part of the funding came from Highland exiles, some of whom made their money, with the assistance of slave labour, from sugar plantations in the West Indies. A year later a Royal Charter was purchased and the name Inverness Royal Academy entered the town's educational vocabulary.

The first Rector, Dr James Weir, was dismissed after just a year as the school entered a fairly scandalous early existence. There is also an account of the sentence "Dulce et decorum est pro patria mori" being belted out on a pupil's hand in the 1870s when he pronounced it wrongly.

In 1895 the school moved from Academy Street to the Midmills building at the top of Stephen's Brae, which inspired this series of books. Here it flourished, initially under an especially successful Rector, William J. Watson. The school continued to expand and extensions were built in 1912 for Science and Art and again in the mid 1920s to give the primary department its own wing.

After World War II, by which time the legendary D.J. MacDonald, who figures prominently in this book, had become Rector, fees were completely removed from the secondary department to which entry was now only on merit. The primary department was phased out in the late 50s, apparently to create more room for secondary pupils, and in 1961 a further extension was opened.

The 70s saw a decade long move towards comprehensive education and in 1977 the Culduthel building opened to this end, with Midmills vacated two years later.

Comprehensive education has continued in that Culduthel building which in turn will be replaced by a new £34.5 million structure in 2016.

PREFACE

From the start I have to admit that the thinking behind this book has rather been a case of putting the cart before the horse! Because what I did first was to decide that I would write it and only then did I begin to think about what I would put in it.

There were two main reasons for changing my mind and deciding to write yet another Stephen's Brae book after declaring the series at an end after "Completely Up Stephen's Brae" in 2009. The principal driving force was that once my retiral in the summer of 2013 became a concrete event in front of me rather than something vague in the future, I felt the need to sign off with one further "USB" volume.

But that third book in the series - the Royal Academy novel "Right Up Stephen's Brae" which catalogues George Fraser's role in the history of the 20th century - has also been a factor. In retrospect it simply doesn't sit comfortably alongside the other two as part of a series and I would like to finish on a more coherent note. At first I believed that an autobiography, an anecdotal history and a novel provided, as they say in football, a "perfect hat trick". But the more I thought about it, the more I came to the view that the fiction which is RUSB, although based on some fact, was really out of step with the other two which describe real life at the school.

So the notion steadily crystallised that I would produce, as my valedictory, a new third element to the real world Royal Academy trilogy, leaving RUSB as a free standing work of fiction. I had even left myself one final degree of ascent of the hill, although, by definition, "Completely" now really must be the last.

But that then begged the question "What do I put in this book?" Well I had for some time wanted to publish brief reflections on growing up in a council scheme in the 60s. It then wasn't very difficult to add to these ideas the extra dimension of going through the Promotion exam system to take one's place in the secondary education apartheid of that era, which included selection for Inverness Royal Academy. I then resolved to make much of the rest of the book a distillation of memories of other FPs. But when the enormity of the task of collecting and organising all of this dawned on me, I was obliged to downscale that part of the project. That was compensated for when ideas emerged for the chapters which focus in on the session 1958-59 and on Midmills' final years in the 70s. Then the news broke that we were to get a new school building to replace Culduthel, so in response I expanded the original content on that, and a book was born.

What I have tried to do is to reflect life at the school from the 1940s through almost to the present day. At the same time I didn't want to duplicate material from earlier books, so the 60s are only lightly covered this time.

I can justify the two "non-Stephen's Brae" chapters on Culduthel on three grounds. Firstly the market for Royal Academy literature, which is not restricted to FPs, has evolved in the 17 years since the original USB and a new generation has appeared. Secondly, the imminent passing of the Culduthel building has to be marked. And thirdly I think that FPs and the general public would actually appreciate an insight into the comprehensive world of the post-Midmills era.

So prepare to share the final - and by far the most varied - insight into life at Inverness Royal Academy.

C.B. – Culduthel. May 2013.

1 - GETTING THERE.

I had my first JFK moment about six years too early. Let me explain. Visits with my mother to her friend Mrs. Reid were never among the highlights of my pre-school days in Inverness. Oh, it was a pleasant enough walk from our house on Kenneth Street, along Young Street with all its little old shops and over the old asymmetric stone suspension bridge, condemned in 1939 but reprieved by the war.

This gave way to Bridge Street, which was still inoffensive and indeed quite pleasant to the eye, with the Burgh Library and Police and Fire Stations tucked in behind. Then to reach the Crown we would enter Castle Street and climb the 73 steps of the Raining Stairs which, at the age of four, I wasn't quite able to count yet.

On the way we might even pass a horse drawn Stratton milk float or a Sunbeam Talbot or a Rover 90 - and very probably also some road works. My mother, who had originally come from Wick, always said that she couldn't get over Inverness's obsession with digging up the streets. Over half a century later, little seems to have changed.

It was only when we got to Mrs Reid's house about half way down the left side of Charles Street that the real problem began. Because once we got inside all they did, apart from drink tea, was to sit and talk which I found painfully boring.

The passage of time means that I can't remember exactly what they talked about. But this was 1957 so the discussion possibly centred on how Mr. MacMillan was doing in Number 10 in succession to Mr. Eden who had made such a pig's ear of that Suez business. Or maybe it was about these six countries which we'd either defeated or liberated during the War signing this Treaty of Rome and forming a new (and for a spell in the 60s, exclusive) club called the European Economic Community. Then in the depths of the Cold War the launch of Sputnik 1 meant that the Soviet Union now in theory had the potential to nuke anywhere on the planet by remote control.

A new television programme called "The Sky At Night" would have been an unlikely topic since we weren't among the 7.8 million households, many of them prompted by the 1953 Coronation, which by that stage owned a TV set and it would be another two years before we did. "Listen with Mother" and "Three Way Family Favourites" on the Light Programme, or "Lift up Your Hearts" and "Yesterday in Parliament" on the Home Service from our large wireless with thermionic valves and stations like Sottens and Hilversum on it were about as much as the Bannerman house had for entertainment in 1957.

Maybe it was a sign of the times or maybe it was just the kind of friends my parents had, but quite a lot of their social life seemed to revolve round sitting in people's front rooms and just chatting. A four year old found this kind of thing intensely boring so, as they chatted on, I found myself drawn more and more towards looking out of Mrs. Reid's front window.

And it was here that I had that JFK moment. You know what I mean. The way you always remember exactly where you were when you experience one of these watershed episodes in your life such as when President John F Kennedy was shot in Dallas in 1963, even though that was still about six years into the future.

"Mum, who are these big boys and girls in these blue jackets outside? Why do some of them have that yellow stuff round the edges?"

So there it is. A crystal clear recollection of exactly where I was and what I was doing when I discovered the existence of Inverness Royal Academy, which would eventually have such a profound and prolonged impact on my life.

I'm not actually too sure how much I made at that stage of the explanation that these were older boys and girls who went to The Academy, which was just at the end of the street, and were on their way home after a day at school. And the concept of an Inverness Royal Academy Prefect which - circumscribed by the first ever issue of silver braid - I would become myself in 1969, would probably have been completely beyond me.

Of Curly, Tomuck, Hairy Hugh and Maude or of morning assemblies and the Smokers' Union I still also knew nothing. The same could be said of Higher French prelims and Fritz's legendary forgetfulness. All of that was still some time in the future but it was at this moment in 1957, eight years before actually walking through the school door for the first time, that the first seeds were sown.

Strong and lasting associations with three famous local institutions have played a large part in my life in the Highland Capital. Inverness Royal Academy is not only the oldest of these institutions but also produced the first and longest of these vital ties. The other two are Inverness Harriers and Inverness Caledonian Thistle, although the athletics club is in one respect the odd one out, being the only one about which I haven't written a book.

There is absolutely no link between my time as a Royal Academy pupil and my later journalistic involvement in football. But it was Bill Murray, that doyen of Royal Academy PE, who did a great deal to point me in the direction of the sport of athletics.

Bill was also indirectly responsible for my first memory of any athletics meeting. It would have been on June 25th 1958 that we walked from Charles Street, past the school, down Lovat Road and the dirt track which

Charles Street today, with the school around the corner on the left.

Victoria Drive still was, to watch Mrs Reid's son Alan take part in the Royal Academy Sports in the school field at the bottom. Amid the sea of regulation white sports clothing, there would again be splashes of that royal blue and yellow since the chosen few selected for the Inter School Sports were allowed to compete in their school vests on their own sports day.

I have no recollection of watching James Wylie going up to collect the senior boys' trophy. But little would I have thought on that midsummer afternoon, that 12 and again 13 years later almost to the day, I would make exactly the same journey myself.

Later parts of this book include reflections of life at Inverness Royal Academy, including some through the eyes of those who attended its Midmills premises at the top of Stephen's Brae. Their memories will be of quite a staid, elitist, conservative, albeit educationally stimulating secondary school environment which at times was quite good at looking down its nose at some of the rest of society. It was also quite easy to succumb to the Ivory Tower mentality and forget that around three quarters of Inverness teenagers lived their lives outwith this exclusive little club to which, before the 1945 Education (Scotland) Act, entry could be purchased, while afterwards it could only be gained through a top performance in the Promotion examination.

At this stage it is still premature to lapse into details of life at the Royal Academy since I am very aware that this account hasn't yet explained how post war youth actually won the right to pass through its portals. So it's now time to have a look at that process of "getting there" and the kind of environment which surrounded it.

Late in February 1965 we were all herded into Dalneigh School's General Purposes Room and given the English and Arithmetic papers which comprised the Promotion exam, along with that epitome of the obscure and the abstract which is an IQ test. This was a procedure which, at the age of 11, would apply an educational label to pupils for life. It was a traumatic experience for many although I have to say that I didn't find it a source of any particular personal angst. Admittedly I was confident of making the grade, and I was also one of these people who actually quite enjoyed sitting exams at school and university.

Unbeknown to us, the Academy teachers marked the papers early in March, which meant their own pupils got two half days. Then, according to the Academy Log Book which records D. J. MacDonald's absences for the purpose, the Promotion Board appears to have met late in April to confirm who was going where.

Formal notification was delivered a few days later so it would have been early in May 1965 that Dalneigh's headmaster John MacLeod arrived in Room 10 to tell Class 7A what their educational fates were to be. And, once embarked upon, these were unchangeable.

There were four categories of course available. The big prize, at least in the eyes of the majority, was an Academic course at the Academy to which sixteen of us aspired. What we also didn't realise until we got up Stephen's Brae that August was that the Promotion performances of the Academy-bound would also determine whether they would be placed in 1A, B, C or D on arrival. At that time, only 1A and 1B were deemed capable of Latin and the rest of the curriculum was also predominantly academic.

The next tier down from the Academic comprised the equivalent options of a Technical or a Commercial course in the High School's "A" stream. This had a much larger element of these named subjects but it was also perfectly possible to do French but not Latin, which everywhere was within a decade of terminal decline, or Greek which was already well on its way out. By now commercial subjects were solely the preserve of the High School and had been discontinued at the Academy in 1949 and although "Tecky" was still on the Academy curriculum, it was strictly confined to being a sideshow in Room 22, with severe restrictions on what could be taught since the High School guarded its near monopoly jealously. Inverness High School also had a reputation for especially tough Tecky teachers who were a dab hand with the belt which added to the attractiveness of a place up the hill where, to us, the staff seemed to be noted more for their eccentricity than their abrasiveness.

Almost without exception Technical and Commercial courses were allocated to boys and girls respectively and, like the Academy, the High School at this level catered for the whole Inverness area. Occasionally the odd poor soul of a boy got sent, or even opted, to do "typeen". Such an outcome was liable to see words shouted after him alleging an orientation, the practice of which in the mid-60s was still a couple of years short of being legal between consenting adults.

Then there was the largest category, the General course for those who had been least successful in the Promotion exam. This was done in the "B", "C" or "D" streams at the High School, or on the other side of the Ness at Millburn Junior Secondary which had opened in 1961 on a site adjacent to the Royal Academy playing field. Here there was a high presence of practical subjects with a lower priority for more academic pursuits, and especially modern languages.

Inevitably the transition from primary to secondary education disrupts friendships, even in the comprehensive era where pupils from one primary school nearly all go to the same secondary but into different classes. When secondary education is selective the rifts are even more profound since groups of friends also find themselves in completely different establishments. As a result, of five of us who had been especially close in P7 at Dalneigh, Brian McBey, Brian Bremner and I found ourselves in three different streamed classes at the Academy while Brian Kavanagh and Derek Barclay went on Technical courses to the High School.

So what was the primary school environment like? I still celebrate the day in October 1958 when my parents collected the keys to 14, St Andrew Drive, a semi-detached three bedroomed wooden Swedish house in the Dalneigh council scheme which had been built in direct response to the post war housing shortage. A stay of over 13 years in Dalneigh, coinciding almost exactly with my schooldays at Dalneigh Primary and then the Royal Academy, gave my outlook on life a very welcome balance. I still love an opportunity to chat about old days there with others who lived or in some cases still live there.

In that connection I will quickly gloss over nicking the Minister's apples, races in the dark across half a dozen back gardens, creating a racket in quiet suburban streets and chucking penny bangers into the front porches of unsuspecting residents under cover of darkness. On one occasion one particularly bold member of our party even installed a

Roman candle in the front hedge of Mrs Anderson, Dalneigh's 5A teacher in St Ninian Drive, lit the blue touchpaper and stood well clear.

Then it would be off to bed to spend time hiding under the blankets, listening covertly perhaps to The Shadows, The Dave Clark Five or The Animals on Radio Luxemburg 208 Medium Wave on my leather cased transistor radio.

If you fancied a swim at the Baths on Friars Place down by the river you could catch the four o'clock bus and Dalneigh School closed at 3:55 to allow that to happen. If you had your "baths card" for one of its squares to be ticked off, entry would be free. After changing in one of the sometimes rather smelly little cubicles, you could prove your virility by swimming a 100 foot length of the pool underwater or diving head first off the 10 foot top board.

St Andrew Drive in 2013 with number 14 on the far right.

If Ronnie Ross or any of the other attendants examined your hands and found your fingers to be wrinkled, the judgement would be that you had been in for long enough and you were sent to change. Then it was upstairs to the canteen for some of those popular tooth destroyers, penny dainties or puff candy, or a bag of Smiths crisps with the blue paper twist of salt in it.

There were also hours and hours of football with jackets for goalposts on the waste land at the back of St Valery Avenue, a universal practice on the part of a generation which is possibly entitled to make a virtue of deploring the unfitness of modern day youth. It was also on that waste land that we religiously built a huge bonfire each autumn, guarding it dutifully at nights in case boys from the Ferry came to cause a premature conflagration.

We would be in Primary 6 or 7, and no parent then in the mid-60s found any cause for concern about us sitting out on a piece of waste land in November with only a small fire, well displaced from the large one, to punctuate the pitch dark. Because this was an era of independence of unsupervised movement outwith the home, even for quite young children. Allowing such freedom would be unthinkable to modern parents, of course, in a totally changed environment.

In the current age of health and safety, it also alarms me to remember the huge stash of fireworks I kept in the cupboard below the stairs of our wooden Swedish house! These were the fireworks which any ten year old could purchase at will over the counter at Toyland in Hamilton Street or from any newsagent.

There weren't even goals behind St Valery Avenue in the 60s!

On then to Saturday afternoon pilgrimages down Balnacraig Road, known to earlier generations of Invernessians as "Bumber's Lane" after an old Merkinch school headmaster. Our destination was the Caley Park where we would climb over the back gate to avoid paying the 9d at the turnstiles before collecting the discarded MacKintosh's lemonade bottles and cashing them in for 3d each at the club shop. Any surplus would go towards the shilling it would cost for the front stalls in the Playhouse or the old fleapit La Scala the following Saturday when Caley were away.

Then a night in would perhaps offer a chance to flick through a large pile of Commando comics. You could buy these admirable publications for a shilling and be sure that decent, upstanding, square jawed British soldiery would always overcome the odds and get the better of nasty Johnny Foreigner. Commando comics were the Empire's response to the transatlantic propagandist myth that John Wayne single handedly won the "41-45 war" simultaneously in the Pacific and in Western Europe while the Brits occasionally helped deal with the Hun.

It was also remarkable how inarticulate the morally inferior enemy always turned out to be. For instance the military might of the Reich never expressed itself more elaborately than guttural outbursts of "Gott in Himmel", "dumkopf", "schweinhund" or at best "achtung Schpitfeuer!" Teutons meeting their ends inescapably did so with an anguished "aaarrghhh!" And in the Pacific theatre, it seemed that the Japs were incapable of any speech at all other than "banzaiii!", whilst uttering the inevitable "aaaaiiieee!" on expiring amid a hail of British bullets. Meanwhile the Italians simply surrendered.

The waste ground at the back of St Valery Avenue, with its thick areas of undergrowth, was also an ideal venue for re-enacting the conflicts of these Commando comics. For hours on end it would resonate to staccato impersonations of machine gun fire from the back of pre-adolescent throats, punctuated by frequent shrill disputes over who was actually "dead".

Then if it was the Victor you were partial to, you would witness the regular eclipse of those slimy, superior, cheating, ex-public school Oxbridge toffs by that decent, fish supper eating, working class hero Alf "Tough of the Track" Tupper. And irrespective of how the toffs had kicked him, tripped him up, stolen his spikes or otherwise conspired to thwart his progress, Alf would always inform them of their competitive demise on the finishing line with an exultant "I've run 'im!!"

This neatly leads me back to the two Royal Academy track championships I've just mentioned. Because the truth is that back in these Dalneigh days I was the only boy to be beaten in the 80 yards by the poor lad who had a slight case of polio and wore a caliper on his lower right leg. Progress to athletic prowess would come later. As a result, the inevitable flight which followed those banger throwing episodes in these early days did tend to cause me some anxiety.

Although this was a time when polio was steadily being conquered by the vaccine in the sugar cube, it had by no means been eradicated. Also in my class at Dalneigh was another pupil whose lower body was completely paralysed by the disease and the girl wore two full leg calipers as a result.

In the Royal Academy log in November 1946 D. J. MacDonald, appointed Rector two years previously and never a devotee of calling a spade anything less than a soil transportation apparatus, uses the alternative term "infantile paralysis" in referring to a Fifth Year girl who died from polio. Then at a time when such things were very much a male preserve, he also records that the funeral was attended by himself, the Boy captain and the boys of class 5C. Polio clearly retained some threat into the 60s since in November 1961 he notes that a Fourth Year pupil suspected of having the disease had been admitted to Culduthel isolation hospital. Even by then, the conventional five letter name was clearly inadequate for D.J. since on this occasion he gives it its full medical title of "poliomyelitis".

To my own great surprise, I eventually mastered athletics and even played rugby in three different positions for the Royal Academy and at scrum half for North of Scotland schools under 15s. But despite having made a second career out of sports journalism and in particular football journalism, I never came to grips in technical terms with The Beautiful Game. This was so much the case that I was one of the smallish minority of Primary 7 boys left to go up to Miss Ogilvy in Room 12 for handwork while the rest got out to play football and contend for places in the school team.

This was an era when Dalneigh Primary had a great reputation across all sports, including a series of really good football teams. I was fortunate enough to source through the school itself the photograph of the 1964 team which I have reproduced on the next page. I was able to name seven of the boys in it and Richard Smith (second right in the back row) was able to provide me with the other four.

Strangely the ones who passed me by included Bill Murray's son Iain (goalkeeper) with whom I played rugby later on and knew quite well, but didn't recognise until prompted. Richard himself became a director of Inverness Caledonian Thistle in 2012 while Sandy Anderson gave years of service to Caley and is now a main stand regular at the Caledonian Stadium. Brian McBey and Brian Bremner, who went on to the Academy in 1965, and Derek Hay were all in that 1964 team whilst still in P6.

The hours and hours of playing at the back of St Valery Avenue and at various other venues across Dalneigh certainly honed the skills and fitness of some of these players. However the author was a lost cause, and invariably a liability for the team who had to take him as "last pick".

Back – Sandy Anderson, Iain Murray, Richard Smith, Peter MacDonald. Middle – Murdo Jessiman, Derek Hay. **Front** – Brian McBey, Gordon Owens, Brian Bremner, Gordon Fraser (capt), Iain MacKenzie, Tommy MacKay.

Dalneigh's main rivals were usually Merkinch whose powerhouse was one Peter Corbett who became one of a select band to play for all three Inverness teams in the Highland League, also managing Caley to the title and becoming Vice Chairman of Clach.

It's worth reflecting briefly on the day in the spring of 1958 when my mother took me to be enrolled by Infant Mistress Kate MacLean at Dalneigh Primary. This was because, after serial visits to Mr. Attwater in the housing department in the Parish Council offices where Johnny Foxes and Jimmy Chung's now are by the riverside, my father was at last on the verge of securing the St. Andrew Drive house. Dalneigh Primary with capacity for 600 pupils in 16 classrooms and its sister establishment Hilton on the other side of the river had quite recently been built to serve Inverness's two major post war housing schemes.

My first impression of Miss MacLean can be summed up in a single word. Scary. This never fully disappeared, although it eventually became apparent that there was a large element of benevolence about the despotism of the woman whom we were obliged obediently to salute each time we entered the building in our lines. My father, who spent the entire war in the Seaforths, probably disapproved of this. Oh not of the action of saluting, but of doing so whilst not wearing headgear, which the British Army always despised as an "American" practice! I don't know if he was aware that when there was another teacher on the opposite side of the corridor, we five year olds committed the even more heinous crime of saluting with both hands at once.

Dalneigh School 2013.

What I didn't know at the time, and indeed didn't discover until I was researching "Up Stephen's Brae" in 1994, was that Miss MacLean's previous job had been Infant Mistress in the Inverness Royal Academy primary department. Then the decision was made to phase that out which meant no more infants there from 1956. So after 10 years at the top of the brae, she transferred to Dalneigh which, although it was not formally opened until 1957, had begun to take pupils three years previously.

Dalneigh in that era was very different from a council housing scheme of the present day, although even then it was still far from being classic Academy territory. In fact possibly only the Crown area could really be described as classic Academy territory, given the school's elite minority status in Inverness and the fact that it was based up there. All the same there were still plenty from the Crown who crossed the Ness for the High School or headed down Victoria Drive or Midmills Road to Millburn Junior Secondary.

In the 1950s and 60s, the overwhelmingly privately owned Crown still owed its strong and long standing links with the Royal Academy to demographic and socioeconomic factors and to the school's now partially receding status as a middle class institution.

Earlier in the educational history of Inverness, class had been one of the main distinctions between the Academy and the High School, which from 1880 until 1937 was situated just 200 yards away in what is now the Crown School. At that point most Academy pupils, apart from bursars, paid fees and hence came largely from the middle classes. On the other hand the High School, known for a period in the mid-20th century as the Technical High School, had no fees so tended to attract much more of a working class clientele.

In "Song school, Town school, Comprehensive", his official history of Inverness Royal Academy, Robert Preece records that when the Academy pupils marched up Stephen's Brae to their new building on the Crown in 1895, they were roundly booed and abused by boys from the High School. This typifies the polarisation in Inverness which continued well into the 20th century, long after real class distinction by ability to pay had disappeared.

I could quote the cynicism - hilarity almost as well - in places within the ivory tower at the top of the hill which greeted news that the "gentlemen's" game of rugby was being introduced to these fellows at the High School in the late 60s. Then in the other direction, it wasn't infrequent to hear Royal Academy pupils referred to, sometimes with justification, as "snobs" - or something worse, perhaps sometimes also with equal justification.

In contrast, attitudes within the Academy to Millburn Junior Secondary seemed different, which creates a strong hint of double standards. Millburn was educationally in theory another step below the High School since it catered only for General level pupils. But despite that there always seemed to be a greater degree of acceptance of Millburn - and of the fact that they played rugby from day one. However, a significant factor there may have been Colin Baillie, who for a time taught PE at both schools and was greatly respected – and, on occasions, feared! – in both as well.

Millburn, unlike the High School, was a new institution so there was no real "history" with the Academy. Furthermore it was also situated in the town's principal middle class area, so many of its pupils were also from that stratum of society. Differentiation with respect to the Academy was perhaps also less acute as a result – maybe even to the extent that it was considered "OK" for Millburners to play rugby.

Whilst discussing issues of residence and class, it's perhaps worth remarking that within Inverness Royal Academy by the second half of the 1960s, I never really detected any class consciousness among the pupils themselves. The fact that I was one of the increasing numbers brought up on council schemes was never a problem with contemporaries whose parents owned their own home in the way that the previous distinction between fee payers and bursars might have been. This also tended largely to be the case by this stage with staff, except perhaps some of the older teachers. Social consciousness, once a major issue, was very much on the wane by this decade of Carnaby Street, Flower Power, The Beatles and the grassy knoll and book depository in Dallas, Texas.

All the same, in Dalneigh, being a pupil at the Academy as opposed to the High School could sometimes be regarded as something of an eccentricity, even in this typically socioeconomically mixed council estate of the mid-20th century.

My father was an Inspector of Taxes, a middle ranking Civil Servant, so had a relatively well paid, professional job. However, with Hire Purchase deemed *infra dig*, that TV, which could also have been rented but wasn't, didn't arrive until 1959 nor the Hillman Minx until 64. The record player came in 67 and we stuck with the council house until 1972. On the other hand the Children's Britannica encyclopaedia, which did so much to develop my general knowledge from the age of eight, was bought the moment the salesman arrived at the door.

My mother going out to work might have accelerated these other acquisitions but in these days married working women, perhaps apart from teachers or the odd doctor, were a rarity and sometimes almost regarded as an admission of failure on the part of the man of the house to provide adequately.

Nor were we by any means the sole representatives of the middle classes in that scheme which, like most similar post war creations, was a very broad socioeconomic church. Just to reveal a sample, within two or three hundred yards of where we stayed there would have been three or four more civil servants of a similar grade to my father. One Dalneigh teacher, Mrs Anderson, lived in St Ninian Drive behind us and two more, plus the Head Teacher of Hilton Primary, were in our street. The Burgh Architect lived through the wall from us and the Firemaster was round the corner in St Valery Avenue while initially Bill Murray, who cycled to school before acquiring the Ford Anglia, was a street away in St Fergus Drive.

So in an era before home ownership became commonplace, there was a much larger middle class presence in council housing schemes. Within 20 or 30 years the next generation of a lot of residents of Dalneigh and other similar developments would own their own homes in Lochardil or Holm Mills, neither of which really existed in the late 50s, or in the Crown.

And therein lies a paradox. Council schemes were far more socially cosmopolitan than they are now. Yet they were such a conspicuous feature of an age when class consciousness may have been under threat, but was still at least alive. Certainly class consciousness had been in the very best of health at Inverness Royal Academy until perhaps the 1960s.

Before that the intake from rented accommodation tended to be looked down on by certain members of staff, compared with those from Central and especially the Crown. That does sit rather strangely alongside the number of teachers who actually lived near us in Dalneigh.

Nancy Scott (nee Sutherland), who gave me an excellent interview for "Further Up Stephen's Brae", did tell me then that she and a number of other extremely able Merkinch contemporaries of the late 40s felt looked on as inferior by certain members of staff.

However, once the payment of fees for state secondary schooling at places like the Royal Academy drifted into history after the 1945 Act, these attitudes changed. One other catalyst for that was the phasing out of the Academy's own primary department during the 50s, although for a short time any need to perpetuate an elite seemed to be transferred to former pupils of Crown Primary.

Given that across Inverness and surrounding area, perhaps up to a quarter of P7 pupils progressed to the Academy in the mid-60s through the Promotion exam, Dalneigh School, with its very broad socioeconomic mix, did not too badly. Of 80-odd pupils in our year, sixteen of us earned the right during the summer of 1965 to go into Johnstone's or Kelly's to purchase that royal blue blazer with the heraldic badge on the pocket which I had first seen from Mrs Reid's front window back in 1957.

On the other hand the Royal Academy's own primary department appears to have done rather better than average in terms of pupils' Promotion exam recommendations for the Academic course. This is hardly surprising since it merely mirrors the trend to this very day of affluence and social class being significant factors in performance in national exams in secondary schools. This was also quite marked back in the 50s and 60s.

Inevitably any primary school's performance from year to year in this Promotion exam would vary. One of several factors was that, with the relatively small statistical sample involved, there would be "good years" and "bad years". D. J. MacDonald only infrequently records in his log success rates in the Promotion exam on the part of the Royal Academy's own primary department. However, in 1957 he does make an exception, possibly for two reasons.

Firstly the primary department was in the process of being phased out and he was maybe making a political point. Secondly, numbers doing well enough to move on to the secondary department appear to have been unusually high that year. On this occasion 24 of the 27 achieved the academic grade which was very high even by Royal Academy standards. But here were the progeny of affluent families educated in classes sometimes of less than 30 as opposed to over 40 in state primaries, so there may be an element of "they would, wouldn't they?"

D.J. also records the somewhat lower but still above average success rate for 1961 on the part of the school's very last Primary 7. Of the 23 pupils, 11 achieved the Academic grade and one, intriguingly after the parents had paid for a Royal Academy primary education, turned their back on an offer to continue into the secondary department free of charge and opted to do a Commercial course at the High School instead. The remaining 11 received General recommendations with one, presumably resident west of the river, going to the High School while the other 10 east Inverness residents would become part of Millburn's very first intake.

What is interesting here is not the east - west imbalance. This no more than reflects typical Royal Academy primary demography. The intriguing observation is the complete absence of recommendations for the middle Technical and Commercial stream at the High School. This may just be a statistical fluke but it may also reflect a talent within the primary department for coaching more marginal candidates in an upward direction for that exam.

The class photo on the page 23 is of Primary 7A at Dalneigh School in session 1964-65. There are some absentees, including Fiona Sutherland and Fiona MacPherson who were two more of five of the 16 Academy-bound members of that class who at some point lived in St Andrew Drive – all in Swedish houses on the same side of the street! The Sutherlands were in number 4, the MacPhersons, then the MacBeys in 8, we were in 14 and Alison MacKenzie lived in number 28, representing an unusually high concentration of pupils in one single year group in the Academy within the Dalneigh housing scheme.

This is because across the piece, Dalneigh kids going on to the Royal Academy were well in the minority, with the overwhelming majority completing their secondary education at the High School, or the "Teckie" as it was still known to many. This was probably more polarised than the likes of the Crown where a larger percentage would be Academy-bound while the rest were divided further by ability between the High School and Millburn JS in a three way split.

In the years following that seminal moment looking out of Mrs. Reid's front window, I became more and more aware of the existence of Inverness Royal Academy and its pupils. There would definitely have been a growing expectation within the family and among friends during my primary school years that I would be going there although my parents' expectations were in no way the product of any pushiness on their part. In an era where everything you did in class was put into a pecking order, it had become reasonably clear at an early stage that I could sustain a place pretty well at the top of it - and hence a desk in the far back corner.

This was a time when, after each term exam, the top pupils were strung across the back row of the class and so on until the lowest achievers found themselves at the very front.

There were of course exceptions since if anyone at the back misbehaved, there would be a rapid, enforced move to the front. I never had a problem here but others were less well disciplined.

The way it fortunately turned out was that in the various tests and exams we had during these Dalneigh days, I always finished a decent second in the class to my friend Iain Steven who in 1965 became Dux while I collected the Proxime Accessit medal. We were both also given the 1963 Promotion papers to try informally in Primary 5. By Mrs Anderson's marking we both passed into the bargain, so there was another quite strong early pointer to the future.

Then when we went to the Academy, we struck another blow on behalf of council house kids. Not only did we both go into the 1A stream, at the end of the session Iain was top of the class and I was fourth and then third in 2A. (I always blamed my total hopelessness at Art, whose inclusion in the pecking order while Music was excluded I always resented, for perhaps denying me better!)

However this was by no means new ground for Dalneigh FPs at the Royal Academy and it had already been outshone. In 1963, Joan Cumming and Helen Smith, who had been three years ahead of us in Dalneigh, took the top two places in the overall Order of Merit for 1A. Further inspection of the 1963 Prospectus also reveals a Dalneigh clean sweep in 1A English where Pamela Beevers pursued these two in third place. It was only later on that I discovered that news of Dalneigh former pupils taking these high places in the top tier at the Academy used to be very well received back at our old Primary school.

So as I progressed through Dalneigh School, it was with a growing confidence that I would be joining the trickle, albeit a bright blue clad conspicuous one, of pupils who would head off on foot or by bike (but seldom by car) along Dalneigh Road and Bruce Gardens towards the Ness Bridge and off up to the Crown. There was a very definite awareness among many but not all parents of Dalneigh's more able pupils that here was a prize – a status indeed – to be grasped with both hands if at all possible. Some would be disappointed but there were also some cases where the Academy place was offered but turned down.

Dalneigh's class 7A – 1964-65

Back row - *Brian McBey, Roddy Williamson, Brian Bremner, Dallas Fraser, John Paul, Tommy Cumming, David Love, Hamish MacMillian, James Findlay.*
Third row - *Audrey Grant, Eileen Ruxton, Catherine Zajac, Linda Mason, Sheila MacIntyre, Lorna Allan, Linda Kirkham, Irene Lilley, Ruth MacKay, Pamela Hendry.*
Second row - *Elizabeth Corbett, Dorothy Fraser, Morveen MacKenzie, Alison MacKenzie, Sylvia Bown, Elizabeth Campbell, Sandra Stuart, Dorothy Duncan, Gillian Diamond, Mary Rooney, Christine Reid.*
Front -*Charles Bannerman, Brian Kavanagh, Iain Steven, Derek Barclay.*

One reason for that was an early acceptance by some families of the harsh economic inevitability that in any case the pupil was going to have to leave school at 15 to seek employment. As a result there was little point in pursuing an academically based course in a situation where the High School might offer better opportunities to take up a trade or an office job in the mid-teens. Then in a few families there was maybe just the feeling that they didn't want their offspring to get involved with "that bunch of snobs".

In reality the Promotion exam, which made a lifetime decision for children at the age of 11, fell some way short of being a precise selection instrument. It very probably got things right most of the time and most of those selected to go to the Academy deserved to do so. But Inverness Royal Academy also received, and was usually stuck with them due to the inflexibility of the system, a number of pupils who really should never have been there as well as the odd complete "dud". Indeed I have heard the conspiracy theory articulated that some of the said "duds" only got there because they had influential parents who could, and did, pull strings.

This lack of "promotion and relegation" also failed to accommodate late developers who were then stuck in the High School. On the other hand it was perfectly possible to do Highers and progress to university from there.

It would be difficult from my own experience to claim that being part of a selected minority was a major problem in Dalneigh. But it would also be foolish to suggest that issues did not raise their heads for Royal Academy pupils from time to time. One factor here was that the dominant secondary educational influence in Dalneigh was most definitely Inverness High School. Apart from well over three quarters of the secondary pupils from the estate going there, the High School was also right on its edge and dozens of Dalneigh kids went in and out through the its back gate on Dochfour Drive.

So it was really a somewhat separate group who made the trip down Bruce Gardens or Fairfield Road and across the river to that large and imposing building at the edge of the Crown. As well as being a separate minority, they were also a privileged one because they were the ones who had been chosen, albeit by ability, for this Academic stream on the other side of town.

I can't say I recollect any huge resentment of that on the part of those not chosen. Others may have found differently but what I saw was mainly an acknowledgement that this simply was the way things were, tempered possibly by mild undercurrents which would occasionally emerge.

"Ach away home an' swot yer Latin!" was probably about as bad as it got - oh... apart from the time I was chased home (fortunately on my bike) by a gang of worthies from the somewhat notorious top end of Laurel Avenue, of whose residents most folk in Dalneigh ran pretty scared.

The fact was that assigning pupils to schools solely by academic selection with no fees was roughly only as recent as the post war Dalneigh scheme itself. Another significant change which came along with the 1945 Education (Scotland) Act was the introduction of what is more generally called the "11 plus" but which was locally known as the

"Promotion" as a means of selecting pupils for Grammar School like institutions such as Inverness Royal Academy. Gone was the system of fees plus County Scholar and similar bursaries for the gifted offspring of the not so affluent. Gone also was the opportunity for a well-heeled family to put cash up front to ensure a place for a less bright sibling.

Part of the preparation for the Promotion exam was previous years' English and, on Friday mornings, arithmetic papers for weeks on end. The 1953 arithmetic paper for some reason was especially straightforward but 11 year olds still had to contend with the likes of complex long division and "if seven men (always men!) can fill a hole in an hour and 20 minutes, how long would it take five men to do the same job?" which is in effect inverse proportion. The problem I always used to have with questions like this was the apparent assumption that "men" always work with equal efficiency in groups of seven compared with fives.

ARITHMETIC TEST – 60s style – see how you get on!

I have made these questions up myself, but very much in the spirit and style of an earlier era and with completely different units of measurement!

MENTAL ARITHMETIC

1) What is the price of 2lb of tea at 1/4d per quarter?

2) How many inches in 1yd 1ft 3in?

3) Find the cost of 3 gallons and 6 pints of paraffin at 6d per pint.

YOU MAY, IF YOU WISH, USE PENCIL AND PAPER FOR THE FOLLOWING QUESTIONS

4) $3\frac{1}{3} + 4\frac{4}{5} - 5\frac{5}{6}$ (answer as a decimal)   5) $5\frac{3}{8} \times 2\frac{2}{3}$ 6) $6\frac{2}{3} \div \frac{3}{5}$

7) A housewife goes into a shop and buys the following – 3 quarts of milk @ 8d per pint, a quarter stone of potatoes @ 5d per lb, 17 feet of elastic @ 9d per yard, half a gross of clothes pegs @ 2d each, a pound and three quarters of mince @ 3/6d per pound. Draw up her bill.

8) A man sets out to paint a wall of his living room. It measures 6 yd x 8 ft. It also has two windows in it. One measures 7 ft x 2ft 6in and the other is 6 ft x 40 in. The door is 6 ft 7 in by 3 ft. Find the area which will need to be painted in square yards, square feet and square inches.

9) A man drives his car for 20 miles at 40 mph then stops for 20 minutes before driving for a further 40 minutes at 60 mph. Find his average speed for the whole trip in mph.

10) A shopkeeper buys a gross of roses at 5d each and 12 yards of ribbon at 5½d per foot. He pays his assistant half a crown an hour for two hours to tie the roses into bunches of half a dozen which he sells for 3/4d each. Find his profit or loss.

ANSWERS.

1) 10/8d   2) 51in   3) 15s   4) 2.3   5) $14\,^{1}/_{3}$ 6) $11\,^{1}/_{9}$ 7) £1 7s 10d   8) 9 square yards, 5 square feet, 108 square inches   9) 40mph   10) A loss of 1/6d.

The only exemption of which I have ever been aware from practising these Promotion papers fell to myself. Mrs. Ballantyne appeared to take the view that I was fairly likely to pass the Promotion anyway - as long as they could read what I had written. However my handwriting was so bad that she thought she could more beneficially direct me towards exercises to improve it rather than persist with sums and essays which I generally found pretty straightforward anyway. As a result I did rather fewer past papers than the rest of the class, being diverted instead to handwriting exercises. I still make a point of boasting that I was the only person in my class at Dalneigh school who ever got remedial handwriting!

My real handwriting nightmare was the mercifully few occasions when we had to practise with old fashioned nibbed pens and liquid ink from ink wells. This must really have been on its way out by now in the early 60s but we still had to do it from time to time. It was awkward enough for the majority but if, like me, you were left handed there were two further difficulties since the world is designed for right handed people. Firstly, since we write from left to right, a left hand goes across the paper after the pen so there was a permanent danger of smudging what you had just written. Then there is the problem that in a right handed world the inkwell was situated at the top right corner of the desk, creating the further risk of a diagonal trail of ink drips across the page.

I often think of primary school handwriting when I am broadcasting to the nation at full time from the Caledonian Stadium or Ross County and get this sinking feeling that there's a word in a couple of lines' time that I'm not going to be able to read. How much more difficult might things have been but for Mrs Ballantyne?

As it happens Mrs Ballantyne, of just three people - all women - who ever belted me, was the also only one who ever made it hurt. Apart from being a very good teacher, this lady could also "lay the belt" and make it sting - even if your hands weren't freezing cold from illegally thrown snowballs!

At this point it's perhaps worth reflecting on how education and society as a whole have changed radically since the mid-20th century in response to burgeoning Political Correctness of one kind or another. Remember that I now write in an era of the European Court of Human Rights and of the Child Protection and "Elfin Safety" industries. Now teachers are encouraged bizarrely to raise a hand in the hope that noisy pupils will do the same and some kind of order will hence prevail rather than adopt the rather more direct approach of bellowing "QUIET!!" (Or alternatively "SHUT UP!!")

Apart from the odd belting, Mrs. Ballantyne also gave me this enormous slap over the head for peeking at the price of my Primary 6 prize, a 7/6d Swallows and Amazons novel. Before she moved on to Fairfield Road and was replaced by Bill Jack the Burgh Architect, Mrs Ballantyne had been our neighbour through the wall and was my mother's friend but that was never going to elicit any favours.

Nowadays of course treatment like that would see a teacher in court, on the front page of the tabloids and defrocked by the GTC. But in the 60s this was perfectly normal and Mrs. Ballantyne was by no means the fiercest. For instance there was Miss MacKay upstairs in Room 13. This was a woman who was universally feared although she did appear to mellow after somewhat belatedly becoming Mrs Ross. She also taught a group which, several increasingly PC revisions later, would not today be called anything like "The Backward Class."

That in turn echoes the 1948 Inspectors' report on the Royal Academy primary department which states in the case of P1: *"Results were generally satisfactory but special measures for the tuition of a retarded section* (sic) *was* (sic!) *advised."* And with P3-5: *"There were relatively small groups of retarded pupils and special measures to ensure their progress were discussed….."* This of course came from an era where the dominant legislation was still the 1945 Act which made specific provision for the education of "lunatics and defectives".

However, even the fierce Miss MacKay would have been trumped by a lady at the Crown School, if her reputation for teaching with the Bible in one hand and the belt in the other was anything other than apocryphal.

By the time I arrived in the Royal Academy in 1965, much of such fierceness as there was in a relatively benevolent regime seems to have disappeared. There were, on the other hand, still tales of the legendary Parrott, the lady Science teacher who was half the size of tuppence and who kept a box in her lab on which she would stand to apply the Lochgelly to her much larger male pupils.

Although the Royal Academy did a huge amount to develop my interests and abilities, the influence of Dalneigh Primary was profound. In particular the grounding acquired there was invaluable.

Firstly there were the basics. Numeracy, helped on its way to a high level by the likes of the mental arithmetic competitions Miss Fraser gave us in P4, was instilled at a very early stage. Then there was that gem of a book called The Essentials Of English. That covered everything from general analysis of sentences to particular analysis, adjectives, adverbs of place, manner and degree and collective nouns such as exultations of larks. My notoriously nitpicking attitude to grammar, sentence construction etc probably has its origins there. That is therefore why I used to squirm at the start of each and every Startrek episode at "to boldly go where no man has gone before." Similarly I could weep any time a footballer, afflicted by "the Glasgow participle" opines that *we should have went ahead.*"

Miss Cameron's folding wooden class library in P3 was an Aladdin's Cave which first introduced me to a love of history. I devoured volumes on the Vikings and the Romans alongside these admirable Ladybird books on personalities such as Elizabeth I, Lord Nelson and Sir Francis Drake. But there was a lot of Scottish content too and it was from Mrs Anderson in P5 and then from Mrs Ballantyne that I learned which of the Kings James had been assassinated or blown up by an exploding cannon or killed at Flodden, which had died in his bed and which gave us the Authorised Version of the Bible.

And a lifelong love of classical music probably has its first origins in the black and white posters Mr Mallinson put up in the General Purposes Room of Vaughan Williams, Mendelssohn and a very grumpy looking Beethoven. They all looked down on us as we took it in turn to come out to the front and point out Psalm tunes in sol-fa on a modulator.

Interestingly there are less detailed memories of subjects in which I found myself less interested. Geography never really appealed to me much, and that was before there was a mutually exclusive choice between it and history at the end of S2. And when it came to Nature Study programmes on the Home Service, that immediately became an opportunity to get a start on that night's homework – probably general analysis tables – in order to create more time for football at the back of St Valery Avenue.

So that was the kind of educational environment experienced by council estate kids who passed their Promotion exam and moved on to the Academy.

An insight into life there begins in Chapter 2 which, as it so happens, concentrated on events at the top of the brae during the very school year that I took my first tentative steps into the infant department in Dalneigh.

2 - A SCHOOL YEAR UNDER THE MICROSCOPE - 1958-59

Many who sat in maths and science rooms during their school days will be familiar with periodic functions such as the sine, the cosine and the tangent which repeat themselves over a fixed interval. Another excellent example of such a function is a school year with its largely fixed start and finish and its regularly repeating features and events as session gives way to session.

By far the best reflection of how year used to repeat on year at Inverness Royal Academy is the school Log Book. Almost a century's worth of them, all in the Rector's own hand from the early 1880s until they were discontinued in the early 1970s, are held in the school archive. But despite the largely periodic annual cycle, there is also a degree of evolution, with slow changes in practice such as dates of national exams and the disappearance of rituals like Promotion test marking and the Installation of the Prefects. There is still a lot of common ground to be found across the entire period during which these were kept – and probably a long time to either side as well.

The log books reach their high water mark under D. J. MacDonald's rectorship from 1944-62 where, in addition to the functional, they become both works of literary art and a vivid record of day to day school life. So my search for a school year on which to focus in detail in this chapter had to be within the D.J era. The quality of the source material was just too good to look elsewhere.

There was another and somewhat more selfish reason behind this decision since D. J.'s handwriting is as crystal clear to read as what he writes is informative and enjoyable. In contrast, on either side of that Crampton Smith's script and especially that of W. S. MacDonald are rather less easily deciphered.

So why, within that D. J. era, have I chosen 1958-59 in particular to focus on? One of the main drivers has been that his log entries for that session seem to excel even by his own supreme standards and a wealth of material, often highly colourful, is available.

It also happens that this session's school magazine, with its relatively new-look blue cover and a large school badge, is one of the best of its kind that I have seen across the decades. Edited by Alexander MacMillan, assisted by Ethel MacKenzie, with committee members Evelyn Cantlay, Rosemary Wright (daughter of Biology teacher Bobbuck), Alastair Morrison and John Murray, this is a truly excellent publication and a fine reflection of school life.

This session also comes at an interesting time in the school's history. Work was beginning on the extension which was to open in a couple of years' time, the running down of the Primary department was ongoing and there were early preparations for what would eventually become the new "O" Grade and Higher qualifications which would replace the Leaving Certificates. There is also an intriguing and continuing interaction between the school and the Inspectorate which at times verges on the intimate during what happens to be an exceptionally interesting session.

In the wider world in 1958-59, ex-Allied Supreme Commander Dwight Eisenhower was in his second term as President of the United States and deeply engaged in the Cold War with the Soviet Union which was testing bigger and bigger hydrogen bombs in the remoteness of Novaya Zemlya. Blue Peter went on television for the first time in October 1958 while into 1959 Fidel Castro and Charles de Gaulle, the latter lionized by head of French Curly Stuart, became Presidents of Cuba and France respectively.

The new session began at Inverness Royal Academy on Tuesday August 26th. This being 1958, it also happens to be the day that my own life as a school pupil began in Primary 1 at Dalneigh. Atypically of the rest of that Royal Academy session, it was quite an inauspicious start in one respect since there were relatively few new members of staff. Ian Milne began in the French Department where that session's new "assistant" was Jean Michel Damiani. The French Department appears to have been expanding at that time because Mrs. Anne Spiers was engaged on a half time temporary contract to fill a void there and started on that day.

Starting also on that August day in 1958, but as a First Year pupil, was Mrs Spiers' son John. Tragically, towards the end of his Fourth Year in April 1962, John Spiers would go on a school Outdoor Club expedition to Stack Polly near Achiltibuie and would be killed in a climbing accident. This tragedy deeply shocked the school.

Miss Elizabeth Morrison had resigned from the primary department back in June on the occasion of her marriage, although since the start of the war such departures had ceased to be compulsory among female teachers. Given that the primary department was winding down annually before disappearing altogether in 1961, Miss Morrison probably solved the problem of which of the four remaining teachers would have to go.

The Log Book also maintains its tradition of recording staff absences, albeit less graphically than in the 1880s when returning teachers had to confess in their own hand to having been indisposed and diverted by the likes of a bout of diarrhoea or indeed writing a speech for the Duke of Edinburgh. But on that first day of the session, D. J. does record that Angus Matheson of the History department was still absent and confined to Raigmore Hospital, suffering from the nowadays very unfamiliar condition of a "tubercular knee".

One member of the new First Year intake was a young lad called Tom McCook who had passed his Promotion at the Crown School to gain selection for the Academy. During his time in school Tom became a passionate convert to athletics after watching Herb Elliott win the Olympic 1500m title in 1960 and in his Sixth Year became holder of the school mile record of 4 minutes 31.2 seconds.

The record which he broke at the school sports in 1964 was that of Royal Academy athletics legend and Scottish schools captain Jimmy Grant who had left the previous June. This is a record which Tom holds to this day since it remained unchallenged right up to 1968 after which the whole system went metric and the mile became history.

After leaving school, Tom moved to Birmingham to work for the Post Office, and married Carol Stewart, sister of world cross country and Commonwealth 5000m champion Ian Stewart whose other siblings Peter and Mary were also international athletes. Over the years Tom would also do service as both chairman and president of Britain's biggest athletics club, Birchfield Harriers.

He has a clear recollection of his preparations to go to the Academy, and how an experience of his own at that time enabled him to save a much younger boy huge embarrassment some five years later.

"I was the first member of my family to go to the Academy and before I first went in 1958, my grandmother said that she would really like to buy me my first blazer," he recalls. *"But then she said she would like to get me one with gold braid round the edge! As it happens I knew enough about the way it all worked to realise that gold braid was just for prefects and people with colours so I managed to put her right on that and it was just a plain royal blue blazer that I got. However, by the time I reached Sixth Year and was house captain of Abertarff with Buckie, I was amazed on the first day of that session in 1963 to see a small First Year boy with none other than gold braid all round his brand new blazer. Remembering my own narrow escape, I very quickly took him aside, told him the way things worked and got him to go straight home to change. I probably saved the boy a great deal of embarrassment."*

By the late 60s, the "powers that be" must have become aware of the danger of the uninitiated creating the heresy of appearing in livery reserved exclusively for the anointed ones and maybe Tom's intervention had played a part in that. Certainly by the time I became a prefect myself in 1969, the only place you could go to have your braid put on was to Kelly's in Union Street and that only with an official chit signed by Bill Murray.

The status of Prefect was one taken extremely seriously by Bill and another of his jobs was to organize their appointment and the conveying of the Chosen Ones to the Rectorial Presence to be informed of their elevation.

PREFECTS 1958 - 59

Back row		J. Jamieson	M. Thom	J. Macdonald		
Middle row	I. Johnstone	I. Macdonald	K. Mitchell	C. Ross	K. West	J. Macaskill
		P. Macdonald	D. Richards	J. Macarthur		
Front row	M. Dilby	R. Lindsay	K. Russell	D.J MacDonald	E.C. Forbes	
	Senior Prefect	*Vice-Captain*	*Captain*	*Rector*	*Superintendent*	
		D. Philip	C.Macgregor	D. Macrae		
		Captain	*Vice-Captain*	*Senior Prefect*		

By the time pupils had returned in that late summer of 1958, work had already begun on the substantial £114,000 extension which within a couple of years would take so much pressure off the three original phases of the building. The school was bursting at the seams to accommodate a roll which had already risen into the mid-70s and would inexorably progress towards a thousand into the 60s.

Inevitably this caused some disruption as workmen descended upon the place and certain parts of the building went temporarily out of bounds or became unusable. However, one can only speculate how the addition of a large extension directly on to the framework of existing premises would have been managed in the modern era of health and safety and whether education could have happened at all in certain areas.

At the front of the Midmills site there was the existing building, the product of three phases of construction between the 1890s and the 1920s, which itself was being changed in places. Now at the back, forming a fourth side of what then became the quad, was the new extension being built directly on to it with a bit of fencing apparently deemed an adequate safety measure. Eventually the men's staffroom had to be "evacuated" on account of the alterations and they had to take occupation of Room 14 instead, the women already having also been decanted elsewhere. Meanwhile some Greek classes migrated to the former second master's room.

The boys' gym had seen extensive alterations and the installation of showers in the changing rooms. This left the boys to change for the duration in adjoining classrooms before undertaking such limited PE as they got at the school field.

Archie Fraser was another pupil who started First Year along with Tom McCook on that August day in 1958. Originally brought up in Balloch, he had to take the bus to school for his first two years before the family moved into Inverness. After leaving in 1964 he went on to do a BSc and then a PhD at Aberdeen University and, a decade after his departure, returned to his old school as Principal Teacher of Biology, having in between taught in Peterhead. As successor to Bob Wright, whose son John was also in that intake of 1958, Archie held his post for three decades. Ironically the turmoil in the PE Department gave him an unconventional and not particularly welcome introduction to one particular aspect of what would become his specialist academic subject.

"When the boys' gym and the changing rooms were being done up there was a long time when the only PE we really got was some cross country at the field, but most of our PE time was spent being taught anatomy by Bill Murray. We were just shoved into whichever classroom was available and to be quite honest, it would have been OK for a period or two but weeks and weeks of that stuff was pretty boring. The front part of the building was totally unaffected when they did the renovations but from time to time the art department was in a bit of a 'boorach' and there were also old outside toilets being knocked down."

The works also saw the removal of a feature of the school's wartime past when, 13 years after the cessation of hostilities, the wardens' post was demolished. During the war, Mr Crampton Smith and then D.J. were obliged to maintain wardens' rotas in the event of fire as a result of bombing. However, in contrast with the likes of Wick and Invergordon which were both military bases, Inverness had remained unmolested by the Luftwaffe for the duration. At the same time the Abertarff gate at the back of the school was removed along with a clump of trees to make room for the new building.

Possibly more ominous even than any threat of assault from the sky is D.J.'s note on October 1st 1958 that: *"Yesterday Miss Young, HMCIS, called to discuss the 1958 SLC (Senior Leaving Certificate) especially in English, History and Science."*

Of most significance is possibly what is unsaid. It has to be inferred that the visit of the greatly venerated local Chief Inspector of Schools then led to an awkward few minutes for the relevant principal teachers Jacob Mowat, universally known as Fritz, and Tommy "Tomuck" Fraser. As well as English, Fritz was then also responsible for History and would remain so for another 12 months until a separate appointment was finally made. Similarly, separate principal teachers in the Sciences were still some time off.

On November 27th Miss Young then returned with one of her subordinates, a Mr Charles Murray, to inspect the Science department and discuss the Science Leaving Certificate results with the Rector and the Science staff. Less than a month later, the Chief Inspector was back again to look at a potential shortage of lab accommodation which had been raised with the Rector by Tommy Fraser.

1958-59 First XI

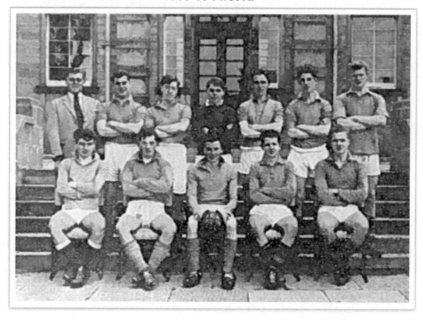

Back row	Mr Cunningham	L Latham	J Urquhart	K MacKenzie
	R MacFarquhar	E Sharpe	G Wallace	
Front Row	J Urquhart	J Summers	D Macrae	
			Captain	
	J Livingstone	J Jamieson		

The name of Miss Edith Young, HM Chief Inspector of Schools, is one which drifts into the log book incredibly frequently around this time. Reading between the lines, there is room to imagine that dealings with this apparently formidable lady, at a time when there were still few women of power about, invariably involved some considerable deference. This was partly a feature of the times, but even when I was a pupil in the latter 60s, there was still this perception of deference – forelock tugging and cap doffing almost – to those in authority such as councillors, the directorate and the inspectorate

One paradox about the elitist Royal Academy is that it also at times simply oozed deference. But this was a protocol which spectacularly broke down on one occasion in particular. Indeed the incident in question may even have originated from Miss Young's September 30th visit to discuss the English results.

I got this story many years ago from Eddie Hutcheon and then related it during the eulogy which I was privileged to be invited to deliver at Eddie's funeral in the Crown Church in March 2012. As an aside, that funeral had an astonishing turnout of former pupils of all generations and of staff whose service at the school went back to the 50s.

The log book records that Eddie joined the staff on September 8th 1958 on his release from military service and what he told me was an anecdote from his very early years as junior member of the department which he would ultimately head from 1968-92.

English, apparently, had received some harsh criticism from Miss Young and this may have been the occasion in question. This had stung Fritz, as principal teacher, to the core. Now at the best of times Jacob Mowat, the bachelor from Orkney whose thick accent sounded so German that pupils thought he was an enemy spy when he arrived in Inverness in 1944, was not averse to the odd hostelry visit. But according to Eddie, Fritz's response to this stinging criticism of his department from Miss Young had been to do a grand tour of Eastgate which at the time was full of establishments such as the Plough, the Albert and the Lochgorm.

Then it gets even better since it would seem that at closing time, which in these days would have been 10pm, Fritz managed to navigate his way up Stephen's Brae. (And in so doing was merely blazing a trail for Oddjob that legendary assistant janitor who frequently made the same transition from Eastgate pubs to the school in the 60s.)

It was then only a few minutes' walk on to Broadstone Park and the residence of the formidable Miss Young. Here Fritz, with his unmistakable Orcado-German delivery, lambasted the Chief Inspector loud and long from the pavement in front of her house for her criticism of the English department at Inverness Royal Academy. What has never been revealed is whether Fritz suffered any consequences as a result of this intemperate outburst. But he certainly remained in post for a further decade until Eddie replaced him, and inherited Room 7, on his retiral in 1968.

One insight into just how formal the whole place was in these days comes from a couple of references to the use of D.J.'s office outwith the school day, which the Rector saw fit to record in the log book. David Thom, then Principal Teacher of Classics but who would become W. S. Macdonald's Depute, was also Principal of the Inverness Royal Academy Evening Institute which offered some valuable adult learning opportunities for many years. Having already recorded permission for use of the school secretary's office beside his own for this after school purpose, the Rector then records on October 10th that *"Mr Thom, Principal of the Evening Institute, now uses my room for interviews on Monday and Thursday evenings when his secretary is here"* (and presumably occupying the office next door).

October 30th provides a log book entry which is of considerable personal interest since it notes that *"the Rector attended the funeral of Miss Mary Jane Campbell, formerly Infant Mistress of Merkinch school."* Carron Cottage, number 70 Kenneth Street, which we had occupied for a couple of years before moving to Dalneigh, had for years been Miss Campbell's home. Then when she was obliged to move into Rossal nursing home on Island Bank Road she had rented it out and we were among the tenants. My mother always had an excellent relationship with "Mary Jane" and I remember being taken to visit this very old lady in her bed at Rossal.

However, her relations, who were presumably set to inherit her estate, were a good deal less charitable and were very keen to get us out – presumably to realise the value of Carron Cottage. Mary Jane insisted that we were not to be moved out in her life time, but the date of her funeral here suggests that we made it by the skin of our teeth since it was in that month of October 1958 that we at last moved to St Andrew Drive.

November 1st was a red letter day for Bill, Buckie and the school rugby club, and if further confirmation of the magnitude of their achievement is needed, it is even recorded in the log that *"The 1st XV defeated Gordonstoun 1st XV by 21:0"* Although D. J. wasn't really an active sports fan, Bill did tell me on a number of occasions that he was very supportive of anything his head of PE ever wanted to do, attended fixtures regularly and was extremely willing to listen to new ideas such as sports colours. He clearly took enormous pride in this victory since sporting references in log books, apart from the Inter School Sports in June strangely enough, are quite rare. That makes it even more strange that the full-page rugby club report in that session's magazine should have no reference at all to this famous victory, but merely records (with uncharacteristically unorthodox punctuation) that *"The 1st XV's fortunes have been mixed – wins just over-weighing losses, but its rugby – open, attacking play - has been, at its best, a delight to watch."*

School log books significantly pre-date the transatlantic litigation culture which would ultimately see ambulance chasing lawyers advertising their services on dozens of freeview channels to clients in the cause of a quick buck. But Rectors still seem to have been very careful to cover themselves in terms of recording accidents involving pupils

Back in the early 20s William Crampton Smith inevitably recorded the incident when Bill MacKell accidentally hit Buxton Forsyth on the head with a metal shot while practising for the school sports. Earlier in the 50s, D.J. also noted that a pupil had put a pin in a schoolmate's food in the dining hall and the pupil was taken to the Royal Northern Infirmary for an X-ray.

In December 1958 he reveals that *"Mgt. Irene Brown of 1B broke a bone in her foot while doing gymnastics with Miss Barrie. Miss Yule* (Maude) *took her to hospital and, after treatment, home."*

Then, a few days later: *"Part of the iron bannister on the lower main staircase snapped this forenoon. No one was hurt but Donald Munro of IIA had the sleeve of his blazer torn. Miss Alexander, Teacher of Needlework, mended it."*

Christmas celebrations started early that year and on December 15th Miss Allan held a carol party in the Primary hall for pupils, their parents and staff.

Then on the 17th, an unusually early six days before the end of term, the school dance went ahead, not in the school itself but in the now long demolished Northern Meeting Rooms opposite Cameron's in Church Street. The relocation had, predictably, been enforced by temporary lack of accommodation in the school itself.

There is an interesting early link between the Northern Meeting, an annual September social gathering of local toffs and their chums, which has now shrunk to little more than a piping competition, and Inverness Royal Academy.

Founded in the 1780s, the Northern Meeting's activities used to include a ball in the Meeting Rooms and a Highland Games which ran for over a century until it went defunct in 1938. For a while in the mid-19th century these Games took place in the school yard on Academy Street but it seems the Royal Academy directors just got too greedy and started charging too hefty a rent. As a result of all this, the Northern Meeting

1958-59 First XV

Back row	Mr Murray	M Thom	W MacKenzie	D Cattenach
	K MacLennan	R Lindsay	P Willis	R Smith
		D Henderson	Mr Buchanan	
Front row	J Grant	J Mathieson	D Richards	D Philip
				Captain
	I Johnson	J MacArthur	D Campbell	

decided to make alternative arrangements and instead built their own Northern Meeting Park on Ardross Street in the 1860s.

The 1958 Inverness Royal Academy school dance, for the Fourth, Fifth and Sixth Years, amid the crystal chandeliered splendour of the Meeting Rooms, must have been a grand occasion indeed. However, one is tempted to wonder how many of the senior boys may have tried to acquire some illicit fortification in "The Gelluns", a mere 100 yards away on Bridge Street?

It is only to be hoped that no one misbehaved as a result of any excessive alcohol consumption since in these days outside guests were invited to school dances. As a result pupils needed to be on their best behaviour – especially on this occasion since it emerges that the apparently ever present Miss Young made a speech on behalf of the guests. Inverness Royal Academy's deference to the Inverness based Chief Inspector of Schools seemingly knew no bounds at this time and I often wonder what Miss Young made of the manner in which she was revered – except by Fritz! On that subject I would also love to know if D.J. ever found out about Fritz's drunken outburst on Broadstone Park and, if he did, how much internal panic and hence need to atone was caused by the thought of offence to Miss Young?

With the pomposity which was to continue to afflict the publication for a few years yet, this was how one male contributor to the school magazine described the other half of the company at that school dance: *"The metamorphosis which overtakes one's female colleagues never fails to astonish; concensus (sic) of opinion from the male side of the hall was that the inclusion of the young and tender fourth was a distinct improvement."*

Christmas at the Royal Academy continued on Monday the 22nd when the junior school held their party in the afternoon and in the evening the choir held a carol service in the Methodist Church, preceded by an afternoon rehearsal. At that time Inverness's Methodist Church was in Union Street but burned down in 1961. This misfortune caused huge distress among Inverness's religious interests.

The congregation decanted for a while to the nearby La Scala cinema until their new premises opened on Huntly Street. The gap site was eventually filled by the building which currently houses the 147 Snooker Club. The term ended on the 23rd in usual fashion with the Christmas concert in the morning in advance of everyone, presumably apart from the Roman Catholic pupils as the next chapter will reveal, piling over the road in the afternoon to the Crown Church. Here the Christmas service was conducted by the Rev George Elliott who had just taken over as minister of Ness Bank Church and hence as school chaplain.

These celebrations, along with delivering the Christmas mail, would have come as light relief for senior pupils who had just finished their SLC Prelims. These took place early in December in advance of the real exams which would continue to go ahead in March before the overhaul of the system which seems originally to have been due around the turn of the decade, but was delayed until 1962.

This brought in "O" Grades which then survived well into the 1980s when they were succeeded by Standard Grade in advance of the minor incursion of intermediate 1 and 2 before National qualifications under the Curriculum for Excellence in 2015. However "Higher" has been sacrosanct as a designation for what is the university entrance gold standard and survives to this day.

It would seem that absence to deliver the Christmas post was simply taken as a matter of course and the Magazine comments that: *"The Post Office's annual S.O.S. did not fall on deaf ears, and the sixth gallantly rose to the occasion. So great were the numbers who answered the call to duty that the services of the fifth were not required, except in the case of one gentleman whose surname luckily began with B. The town was filled with long-striding types dressed in Outdoor Club attire, in some cases down to Commando-soled boots, weighing three pounds apiece."*

When the new term began on Monday January 6th 1959, alterations once again loomed large, with Bobbuck Wright eventually forced to abandon Room 30 mid-lesson when its occupants were overwhelmed by dust from a grinding machine on the ground floor. But there is also a reference to the school field requiring to be partly dug up to install a cable *"to supply the new 'Scotsman' building with electricity."* I take the premises in question to be the now demolished low brick building between Diriebught Road and the field which for many years housed Highland Printers, including that Inverness institution the Football Times. But it does seem rather large for a local office of The Scotsman, although it may have been a case of shared use – unless D.J. simply got his facts wrong, which was unusual.

It may have been the cold snap which resulted in country pupils being sent home early for fear of snow on January 23rd that started it, but by the 27th, something of an epidemic was gripping the school. The log book records: *"Heavy absences owing to a feverish cold, with sickness. In Hedgefield girls' hostel there are 23 cases and 12 in the Drummond Park boys' hostel."*

But then the next entry for the 28th reads: *"In the afternoon, 300 pupils from the school went to the schools' matinee of the Scottish Orchestra. Mr. Murray, Principal Teacher of Physical Education, took charge of the party. V and VI were kept in school for the SLC studies."*

1958-59 Hockey Team

Back Row	S Hamilton	R Foster	A Urquhart	J Murray
	A MacIntosh	H Lyon		
Front Row	J Garrioch	J Campbell	K Russell *Captain*	Miss Barrie
	D Hamilton	J Cumming		

This prompts one or two interesting observations. Firstly, in the throes of an infectious epidemic, 300 pupils still seem to have been sent to what one assumes to be the massive (and often freezing cold) Empire Theatre where cross infection must have been rife. And here is yet another example of the plethora of odd jobs, ranging from setting out the exam desks to operating the Prefect system, which would be undertaken by Bill Murray for almost another 20 years. Then there is the apparent contradiction of senior pupils being allowed out of school to deliver Christmas mail, but not for a single afternoon's far more educational orchestral concert.

February saw the advent of a period of frequent brushes with the law, with police recorded as having visited the premises on no fewer than five different occasions within two months. Three of these visits involved break-ins at the school, although nothing of much consequence was ever taken. The first, on Sunday 1st February 1959, saw the removal from the Lady Superintendent's room of several items including a travelling rug.

Then on February 28th or March 1st a French dictionary was taken from Room 15, vice-captain Robert Lindsay's books from the boy prefects' room, and from Room 20 – a tawse. Soon after, Bill's store was deprived of a cricket bat and ball and a pair of tennis shoes. Between burglaries, on 9th February a police constable interviewed a First Year pupil who had allegedly been assaulted on Southside Road the previous Saturday.

But as March entered its final week, investigations became a good deal more internally focused. On March 24th: *"At the change over from period 6 to period 7 Miss Barrie, Assistant Teacher of Physical Education reported the loss of her gold wristlet watch, which she had left on the window sill of her gymnasium. The Rector reported the matter to the Police. Sgt. Aitken and Constable Ross visited the school about 3:45 and saw Miss Barrie."*

Then the following day: *"Police Constable MacKay and Policewoman Sutherland spent most of the morning interviewing the girls of 1cd and 2ab about Miss Barrie's watch. Miss Cuthbert was 'in loco parentis' during the interrogation in the Lady Superintendent's room."*

However in that era of Juvenile Courts, it is not known how or whether this issue was resolved since there is no further reference to it in the log book.

It seems that a cold snap also continued into February since on the 5th it emerged that *"The outside Lavatories (D. J.'s capital "L") are frozen. The boys are restricted to one lavatory inside the main building because the Midmills Road side lavatories are not yet ready."* Two weeks later this crisis would deepen since *"the school was without water since a mechanical digger, engaged in the building operations, cut through the main."*

Also that month there was considerable extra-curricular success outwith the world of sport since Kenneth MacKinnon of the Fifth Year won the boys' prize in the Toastmasters' speech contest. Then Mrs. Spiers' road safety quiz team of Donald MacMillan, Sandy MacDonald, David Watson and Alastair Wingate of IIIA won their event too.

The Road Safety Quiz for what the magazine, in the pre-Millburn age, describes as *"local youth organisations and the two secondary schools"* was held in the Cameron Highlanders' War Memorial Boys' Club and won by a single point from the Girl Guides.

With V, VI and VII still making their way out of the primary department before it closed in 1961, the Academy joined with the other primary schools in town and throughout the County to host the Promotion Exams on Tuesday and Wednesday February 24th and 25th. No time was wasted in marking these exams and intelligence tests, and on the following Monday and Tuesday, March 2nd and 3rd, the Academy's secondary pupils got their customary half days for staff to mark the papers from across the area.

Come August, these exams were planned to provide the school with by far its biggest intake into First Year - 190 pupils which was 50 more than had ever been admitted before. This substantial increase may have signified a change in admission policy. But might one further factor have been some spike in the post war baby boom corresponding to 1947, following large scale demobilization? At a time when accommodation was stretched amid structural change and turmoil, this was a brave move to make so early. In the end it appears that rather fewer than 190 were admitted, but the accommodation difficulties were still severe when the new intake arrived.

Also on March 2nd the Leaving Certificate exams began. The Chief Supervisor (now called invigilator) was the Rev Donald MacFarlane of the East Church and his assistants were Miss Urquhart, Miss E. Cameron, Mr MacMillan and Mrs Louise Robertson. A decade later, by then into April and May, I sat my own "O" Grades in the new hall which in 1959 was still under construction. I have a clear recollection of Mrs Robertson still there, as fierce as ever and now as assistant to Buxton Forsyth's former shot putt assailant Bill MacKell. The SLC Exams continued until the 20th when Art brought the curtain down. In the intervening period the programme had encompassed not only the commonplace but also the now disappeared subjects of Analysis, Botany, Dynamics and Greek.

On March 26th the Rector held an end of term staff meeting where the building works were inevitably on the agenda. But so also was the announcement that the "Fourth Year certificate examination" - what would eventually become "O" Grade - had been postponed. Until that point there had been various references to preparations for it, including inevitable consultations with Miss Young. But now this significant innovation would not see the light of day until 1962.

Alec Munro must have been a happy man that Easter of 1959 because at last he was to be rid of the idosyncratic coal fired heating system and its filthy fuel. During the holidays the entire system was removed but there would be a long delay before the new oil fired one would be up and running that October. Unfortunately the weather turned chilly in the interim and on May 4th *"to meet the cold, owing to the removal of the old heating system, Mr MacDonald, Assistant Director of Education, supplied three oil heaters, which the Rector placed in the junior school rooms."*

The following day Mr MacDonald sent up a further half dozen heaters and the Rector borrowed four more from Fraser and MacColl the well known ironmonger in Eastgate.

One can only assume that the Messrs MacDonald, Rector and Assistant Director did not perform these tasks personally. But, even if they only facilitated them, this is another insight into the relatively mundane matters dealt with directly by the holders of quite senior posts in these days.

Back in 1937, Ronald MacDonald had been one of a number of Hostel boys quarantined in Drummond Park due to scarlet fever. Two decades later this FP had become Assistant Director, which was the "number three" behind the Director Dr MacLean and his depute Alan Lawson. Mr MacDonald later moved into the top job and became Inverness shire's Director of Education.

After it became redundant as a coal cellar with the change of heating arrangements, the space beneath the boy prefects' room, which was accessed by a stairway opposite the boys' toilets, then became a Sixth Year common room. This dark and dingy grotto was also where I learned how to play the clarinet - badly I would have to emphasise. Confronted with the hopeless task of teaching me was that legendary Capstan Extra Strong chain smoking ex-army bandmaster Fred Short who arrived during the late 60s as the school's woodwind instructor.

Fred was a tremendously talented musician with a great flair for arranging as well as teaching and along with all of that he also became a guidance teacher at the school during his latter years in service. His army background was probably ideal for all these functions.

However, the seeds of his appointment were sown in 1959 and on March 4th D. J. reveals that: *"Mr J. L. MacAdam, County Music Organiser, discussed with the Rector the formation of a class for the teaching of wind instruments."*

At that time Jimmy MacAdam was also organist at St Columba High Church where his mother was a member of the congregation and a Sunday morning would not be complete for me without a wink from Mrs MacAdam. One of his successor organists would be David Hardie, who was the son of the diminutive "Ma" Hardie of the Maths Department and who would become dux of the Royal Academy at the end of that session 1958-59.

David Hardie was a major figure in Inverness music circles for a time in the 70s and one of his enterprises was called "The Sine Nomine Singers". Now that's simply Latin for "without a name", but for many non-classicists how it should be said was a problem. Frequently the pronunciation you would hear about the town suffered from the same error as when someone given an indefinite ban is (phonetically) referred to as having been "sign dyed". But the Sine Nomine singers, including not a few former Royal Academy pupils, were something of a musical institution around Inverness.

Primary 7 1958-1959.

In his organist days, David Hardie also became famous for nipping along to the Cummings Hotel in Church Street for a dram during the evening service sermon (and there would be no shortage of time!) When the minister got to hear about that destination, he first thought it wasn't too serious a problem that the organist should pop out for a soft drink - until he was put wise that the "orangey" he thought was involved was in reality a well-known whisky distilled in Tain!

Student teachers have been in and out of schools almost since time began, but they are not very frequently referred to in the Log. However on April 15th, the Rector tells us that: *"All this week Mr Renato Ferrari has been doing teaching practice in the French Department."* Within a very few years his sister Leonella, Mrs Longmore, would join the staff and remain for about quarter of a century before retiring as Principal Teacher of Modern Languages, a post she would inherit on Curly's retiral in 1973.

In 1959, Fritz was finally relieved of responsibility for History when the long overdue appointment of a separate Principal Teacher was made. During the summer term there seem to have been extensive discussions about this involving the Rector and the directorate and of course the entire proposal just had to be run past Miss Young. It almost becomes worth asking who was running education in Inverness shire at this time – the Director or Miss Young? Eventually, in October, Farquhar Macintosh took up the post. He would stay for four years before leaving to become Rector of Portree High School and then of the Royal High School in Edinburgh.

One other regular feature of the summer term was the annual Inverness Music Festival in which Jimmy MacAdam and his successor Music Organiser, Curtis Craig, were extensively involved. Here we can rely on the school magazine for this revelation in an era when much of the training of Royal Academy pupils for the festival would have been undertaken by Principal Teacher of Music Laurence Rogers who was never known as anything other than "Boosey" which, it should be explained, is a reference to the music publishers!

"The first contingent from the Academy, some sixty strong, arrived at the Empire Theatre on May 26th, and had the hazardous honour of opening the Music Festival. Thereafter the familiar school colours were never absent for long from the platform, either in school entries or in general competition. Owing to some slight loss of pitch, the mixed-voice choirs did not quite come up to last year's standard, but the mixed voice quartets, four of them, provided, according to the adjudicator, Mr. Cedric Thorpe Davie, one of the most enjoyable classes in the Festival, and the quartet had the honour of being added as an extra item at the final concert on Thursday night. Space does not permit, as usual, mention of all the various successes, but in open competition, Isobel McConnell won the under 18 vocal solo with Christine Wood a close second."

What this doesn't mention, but the log book does, is the new School Orchestra which performed for the first time on the final day of the festival on May 28th. Trained by Miss Isobel Bethune and conducted by Jimmy MacAdam, it performed the Toy Symphony with seven prefects playing the "toys" which unusually have parts. D.J. refers to the work as Haydn's but in the intervening years it has become attributed to Leopold Mozart, the father of Wolfgang Amadeus.

Cedric Thorpe Davie was a revered figure at the music festival for years. Professor of Music at St Andrews University, he was a prolific composer, his works including scores for a number of films, and he was much sought after as a judge at events like this. Also greatly sought after were invitations to perform in the festival's final concert. During Fred Short's time it was almost inevitable that the Inverness Royal Academy orchestra would receive such an invitation to perform one of Fred's legendary arrangements of the likes of "Lily the Pink" or "Dr Zhivago".

Guest speakers were, as always, regular visitors to the school and the second half of May seems to have been especially busy. On the 19th, Lt. Cdr. Barry RN spoke to about 40 senior boys about careers in the Navy and a couple of weeks later the army and the WRAC would have their chance to tout for well-educated recruits. On the 20th, Lt. Col. Callander of the SSPCA addressed Primary 7 on "Kindness to animals" while on the 26th it was the turn of Prof W. M. Smart of the Chair of Astronomy at Glasgow to give the annual Cormack Lecture. His topic was atomic energy, with Principal Teacher of Geography Frank Cunningham in the chair. This was an especially appropriate subject at the end of a decade which had seen prototype reactors constructed at Dounreay in Caithness and Windscale in Cumberland. Windscale, where there had been a serious nuclear accident just two years previously, was later renamed Sellafield.

The day after that it was the turn of a Mr Patel, a Ugandan Asian science teacher, to visit that department while Mr Cunningham presided over another lecture. This time the visitor was the colourfully and somehow appropriately named Sir Hilary Blood, former Governor of Barbados, whose subject was the West Indies.

There was a major drama on June 12th 1959 when the Hill Park Roman Catholic hostel, which was part of the Convent of La Sagesse, was destroyed by fire. The convent was on the corner of Southside and Culduthel Roads and the site of the adjoining hostel later became St Ninian's Catholic Church on Culduthel Road. It must have been a sudden and serious blaze since a nun and a 13 year old pupil, not apparently of the Academy, broke bones falling whilst escaping from a 30 foot window using a rope improvised from bedsheets.

Three pupils of the Academy - Mary Flora MacKinnon, Mary Flora MacNeil and Katie MacNeil, predictably from Barra - and five High School pupils lost all their belongings in what was very much an emergency evacuation. The log book tells us that: *"All were housed in Hedgefield till able to go home and clothes were provided by the Hostel girls and by the W.V.S."*

At least if the SLC exams were early, so were the results and on June 15th it emerges that 116 new Leaving Certificates had been gained with 65 pupils adding to subjects passed the previous year. One wonders what on earth pupils, especially in Sixth Year, did after sitting these exams in March in an era when staying on until the end of the session was compulsory?

David Thom seems to have been seeking promotion at this time and on June 17th was absent being interviewed as a possible Rector of Wick High School. He was unsuccessful and three years later the Principal Teacher of Classics would become Second Master at Inverness Royal Academy in succession to "Pop" Frewin - a post Mr Thom then held until his untimely death in service in December 1970.

The second half of June takes on an unmistakable flavour with so many of the end of term rituals set to be played out. On the 19th the Rector and heads of department decided that David Hardie would be Dux and Alistair Morrison from North Uist the proxime accessit. Four days later they resolved to award the Howden Gold Medals for Honour to girl captain Kathleen Russell and boy vice-captain Robert Lindsay, which he may have found was some compensation for the theft of his books.

The penultimate Wednesday of June - in this case the 24th - was always the traditional date for the School Sports and on this occasion the champions were Roddy MacFarquhar and Janet Campbell. The awards were presented by Mrs Donald Duncan, wife of the local solicitor who was a regular official at the sports, a major player in the North of Scotland AAA and President of the Scottish AAA in 1957.

No doubt the meeting, with Buckie's voice booming out over the tannoy, would have gone ahead with its usual military precision under Bill's stewardship. This, a year in advance of his inspiration by Herb Elliott, would be the first experience of a school sports for Tom McCook but there would be little on the programme to interest a First Year pupil whose talents lay in the longer distances since Bill was still quite conservative about whom he allowed to participate in this area of the sport.

Inverness Royal Academy sportsday was always a huge occasion in the school year, with a vast amount of work doneby Bill Murray and many other staff to ensure that the day went off without a hitch. And, apart from the big unknown of the weather, it invariably did.

Inevitably at this stage of the session staff departed and as early as June 5th Mrs Flora Clark, teacher of what would be the last Primary V, left her post. It looks likely that she would have been out of a job in any case at the end of the term since the Primary Department would then reduce to just the top two years. She may therefore have taken an opportunity to move elsewhere and was presented with an air travelling case on leaving. However the main bulk of the departures took place right at the end and on the second last day of term, July 1st, the school closed at 3:20, the end of Period 7, for staff presentations. Those listed as leaving are Miss E. Jean Alexander (Needlework), Miss Mary I. MacPherson (Geography) and Angus Matheson (History).

Then on July 2nd the session came to its familiar close when the school crocodile marched down to the Playhouse cinema which by now had succeeded the Empire Theatre as the venue for the Prize Giving. Once again education committee vice chairman Col K.P. MacKenzie was in the chair.

Adverts - 1959 Magazine.

So who was 1959's much deferred to Chief Guest Speaker and presenter of the prizes on this prestigious and very formal occasion?

Yes, you've guessed! It was Inverness education's very own "rent a celeb" Miss E. Young HMCIS, who must surely by now have been getting to some stage of embarrassment at the abject sycophancy coming in her direction from Inverness Royal Academy.

Unwritten school policy or a subconscious expression of guilt following Fritz's alcohol fuelled indiscretion?

These last pages have been just a snapshot of daily life at the top of the brae during just one, albeit an especially interesting one, of the 84 sessions when the school was based there. Other years will bring forward other pupils' memories which are at the same time similar but distinctly different. The next chapter takes a look at just some of these memories.

3 - RANDOM REFLECTIONS OF SCHOOL LIFE

What follows is a series of insights into school life from the mid-1940s through to the early 70s, where Chapter 4 then takes over. These begin with a distillation of what emerged from a series of interviews I did with former pupils and staff. Many of these came in response to an appeal I made for memories when I decided in the summer of 2012 to go ahead with this project. Then we move on to further gleanings from D.J.'s Log books which are just too good a source to fail to exploit to the full.

The first set of recollections is also the earliest and includes an insight into what the school was like in wartime and also under the rectorship of William Crampton Smith who was in charge from 1920-44.

Angus MacKenzie was a pupil from 1943 to 1949. His family initially farmed at Meikle Kildrummie near Nairn before moving to Drumine at Gollanfield and he had his primary education at Croy. When the time came to move on to the Royal Academy, he boarded an Alexander's bus into town at ten past eight every morning and was on Eastgate by 8:45 for the short but familiar walk up the hill. A stalwart of school rugby teams, he has fond memories of the bus home departing at 4 o'clock so he and a number of fellow travellers from east of Inverness were allowed daily to leave class 10 minutes early at 3:50.

Angus went on to qualify as a Chartered Accountant in Edinburgh in 1956. However he always wanted to return to Inverness and soon after doing so, set up his own firm of Angus MacKenzie and Company. It now practises as MacKenzie Kerr and operates from the former La Sagesse convent referred to towards the end of the previous chapter. His memories of Crampton Smith, the deeply religious scout leader who retired when Angus was in First Year, are relatively positive. Others have been less generous. But, as we shall see, the real hero for Angus was D. J. MacDonald with whom he forged a strong lifelong association.

"I found Mr Crampton Smith to be a very pleasant but austere gentleman," he told me. *"I have no recollection of him speaking to me but I don't see why he should. I would never have approached him myself because he was superior to us but I believe he would have been very approachable if necessary. We held him in the highest regard but he had a much quieter presence than D.J. did and was much respected by staff and pupils."*

Perhaps it was because he only came into First Year in 1943 when the war had just two years to run and its tide was beginning to turn, but Angus remembers relatively little educational disruption as a result of the hostilities.

"Really we didn't know that there was a war on in school although were aware that some pupils had left and had gone off to serve in the forces.

From the point of view of our own teaching and sport, things went on as normal. Even school meals were good and that's coming from someone who was brought up on a farm when we had a good supply of food by wartime standards. I have no memories of firewatchers on the roof or even of sandbags in the building although they must have been there. But I do remember carrying our gas masks in a square cardboard box and the occasional gas mask drill.

"Inverness itself wasn't bombed although they did try to hit the aluminium works at Foyers. One German plane failed to find the target and jettisoned its bombs at Stratherrick and many years later I saw the craters. Dalcross airfield was just across from us and it was a gunnery school. Our farm looked over it and on two occasion aeroplanes – a Whitley bomber and a Harvard trainer - crashed. I remember seeing all the guns and bullets in the Whitley but two men were killed in the Harvard so my father wouldn't let us near that."

While Angus was pursuing his C.A. qualification in Edinburgh in 1954, one of his former neighbours joined the Maths department at his old school. Patsy Forbes' family ran a nearby farm at Little Kildrummie, and she would continue to live on it for many years before finally moving into Nairn itself. She is remembered by generations of pupils as the leading light in the Country Club which she ran from 1956 until she retired in 1990. This Royal Academy institution, which is the only extra-curricular activity I followed for my entire six years as a pupil, was unique since it was a Young Farmers' Club but based in a school. This extremely popular club, which inspired huge loyalty from its members, enjoyed a great deal of success over the years and celebrated its silver jubilee in 1981 (see Chapter 6).

Patsy was also a keen supporter of the Outdoor Club where she says some great friendships were started and, as recently as 2009, there was a 50th anniversary lunch for some of the survivors of a legendary 1959 Outdoor Club foray which had also included Patsy's fellow mathematician Janet Banks, Frank Cunningham and Alastair Gammie.

In 1958 Patsy was still a couple of years short of having her own classroom so was defined as "peripatetic" within the building. Deriving from the Aristotelian tradition of walking about whilst teaching, peripatetic teachers, who were usually recent arrivals, were by no means uncommon at Midmills. Patsy was also one of three "Misses Forbes" on the staff, but does not remember any great confusion.

"There was Ethel Forbes who like me was in the Maths department as well as being Lady Superintendent and there was also C.D. Forbes in French so I was simply known as 'Miss Pat Forbes' and that sorted it all out. For my first six years until the new extension opened I never had my own room and taught in various rooms about the building. That included a *former primary classroom beside their assembly hall but that was converted into changing rooms for the girls' gym.*

"At one point I had a Fourth Year arithmetic class with 68 pupils in it so all we could do was to split them between two classrooms and I would teach something to one half while the others worked and then I would change round and do the same lesson again with the other half. There was no problem with the group I had to leave because in these days discipline wasn't really a problem. I was moving about all the time but didn't have a cupboard although what I was given to teach with were four books on Algebra, Geometry, Trigonometry and Arithmetic, a box of chalk, a blackboard duster and my marks book so there wasn't too much to carry around the building.

"Sometimes you would go into a class and not know whether you could rub off whatever someone else had on the board and that was especially true in Geography where you had to be careful not to rub off one of Frank Cunningham's maps. Sometimes I used a separate blackboard and easel to avoid problems. When the new building opened in 1960 the primary corridor also became the girls' wing and a room for Domestic Science, Room 35, opened there. As a result Room 2 at the front of the building, which had been a sewing room, became vacant and that then became my maths room so I then had a place of my own for the first time."

Patsy, who remained in Room 2 until the 1979 departure, also has a clear memory of the period in the late 50s when the building works were under way and recollects that the disruptive effects were quite patchy.

"Most of it was going on at the back of the building and away from the rest of the school but there was also a lot of work taking place in the primary department where there were a few changes and a few other places. The front part of the building really wasn't affected at all and the partitions that went in to convert the old hall which had all these benches for assembly into the library weren't put in until after all the rest of the work was finished and the new assembly hall at the back was in use."

Another of Eddie Hutcheon's anecdotes tells of the period when music classes were occupying the old hall along with an inevitable piano. On that piano, Jess Thomson placed and lovingly tended a flower – until the day when someone cut the head off it. The fuss she made to D.J. and the resulting inquest became the talk of the school for some time.

Ian Philip spent 10 years as a pupil from 1945-55 where his contemporaries included Donald MacBean, John Urquhart, Alastair MacLeod, Isla Rose and Maureen Munro. He went straight into Primary 2 (the equivalent of the modern P4 since it was preceded by two years of Infants) from Culduthel School where he began his education because the family home was at the time close to Culduthel Hospital on the very edge of town.

He left the Royal Academy as Captain of the School and of the 1st XV and went on to Aberdeen University where he studied Civil Engineering. Ian worked in a variety of locations, including for a while for Wm Tawse Ltd where his father had earlier been a senior figure, and he eventually formed his own company. Ian now lives in Kincraig near Kingussie.

As a prominent rugby player he was very much one of "Bill's Boys", as was his brother David who followed him in both captaincies four sessions later in our featured year of 1958-59. Interestingly enough, although they were both long gone by the time I became a pupil, it was from Bill Murray that I first heard of the Philip brothers. Back in the 60s the old blaes Queens Park running track was fast becoming unusable for lack of maintenance because the management committee, of which Bill had been a founder member, had gone defunct.

When I was at school, Bill explained to me that back in the mid-50s when it was built, the father of two of his rugby boys, the Philip brothers, was with Wm Tawse. It was through him that arrangements had been made to install the bottoming for the running surface. Bill assured me that, although the top surface was rapidly deteriorating for lack of care, the base was still very sound - and so it transpired. Because as late as 1984 when the current all-weather track was laid at the Queens Park, the existing bottoming was so good that it was just kept there, saving a lot of money on the contract.

Ian's Royal Academy memories begin in the primary department in the dying days of World War II which saw allied forces well on their way towards Holland and the German frontier.

"On my first day at the school in 1945 when I would have been about eight, my mother took me down from Culduthel on the bus and we walked the rest along Southside Road. I decided to go in through the front door on my own. But when I did so, all I saw was this man in a gown, who of course was D. J., and literally hundreds of faces, so I just turned and ran back down the path. That was my first experience of Inverness Royal Academy.

D. J. MacDonald.

"Alice Grant was head of the primary department and was a very tough lady but an excellent teacher. We had her in Primary V which was our last year before secondary and she was unusual for a primary teacher in that she wore a gown. She was very much in control and wasn't afraid to use the belt. All the boys got the belt but I don't remember at any time in the Academy any girls getting it. At Culduthel School it had been a lot

harder than that because you could get the cane across the knuckles and anyone who lied had to wash their mouths out with soapy water.

"The Academy boys also had to wear caps and if you met a teacher when you were wearing a cap you had to salute - but only if you were wearing the cap as was the case with the British forces. Then during the Victory celebrations we had a presentation of gifts up at Culduthel and when I went up for mine, going by the rules we followed at school, I didn't salute and I got a real row for that, even though I tried to explain 'but I wasn't wearing my cap!'

"Although I was captain of rugby I did play a little bit of football and when we moved into town and stayed on Kingsmills Road I actually once played in goal for Thistle 2nd XI so I do like to think I have that slight link with Caley Thistle. A lot of footballers played rugby as well and certainly at that time I wasn't aware of any tension in the school between rugby which was run by Bill Murray and Buckie the art teacher and football which Frank Cunningham the Geography teacher looked after. I think at that time Bill was just trying to build rugby up although he was also excellent with athletics. I played in the game in 1953 when we beat the Abbey 33-0 and Sandy Sanderson ran in six tries and my brother was captain a few years later when they convincingly beat Gordonstoun.

"If it was a cold winter, it would be quite normal for the toilets to freeze over. They were just lean-to structures against the main building at that time, and Mr Munro the Janitor was great for catching boys smoking in the toilets.

"Another memory I have is of sharing Buckie's enthusiasm for the Goon Show which had people like Harry Secombe, Spike Milligan and Michael Bentine in it. This was a radio programme on a Monday night which was extremely popular in the 50s and on a Tuesday lunch time a few of us would go into Buckie's art room to discuss the previous night's show. That was part of the great camaraderie we had in our year at the school. It was second to none and you would have died for some of them."

Hugh Grant from Beauly had his final three years of secondary education up the brae from 1953-56, having begun that at the now long-closed Junior Secondary in his home village where he passed an entrance exam for the Academy. His fellow travellers into Inverness in the morning included Duncan Michael, later Sir Duncan Michael, and Chairman of the civil engineering firm Ove Arup.

After leaving school, Hugh did three years' National Service in the Parachute Regiment. He then shelved plans to go to university when a temporary job as a trainee manager in the Caledonian Hotel diverted him towards a lifetime in hotel management, including many years in charge of the Drumossie. He remembers this rare encounter on arriving in Inverness en route to school one morning in his Fourth Year.

"Quite a few of us came in by service bus from Kirkhill, Beauly and all points north. We were decanted in Academy Street and it was a mad dash for Stephen's Brae with the bell tolling to make it in time for assembly. One day a group of us emerged from Hamilton Street into Eastgate heading for school when we saw a wondrous sight! Four Celtic footballers were standing on the pavement, immaculate in their green club blazers and matching trousers. They were halted looking about with rolled up newspapers in their hands; the previous evening Celtic FC had come north to play Inverness Caley in a friendly match. Now as you can guess, we were totally unused to bumping into such stars in the douce streets of the Highland capital. The players in question were Jock Stein then a craggy centre-half for the Hoops, Bobby Evans, Charlie Tully and Sean Fallon.

"We crossed the street so as to get closer to our heroes. Then Jock Stein spoke to us directly 'Hey son, is there a bookie's round here?' Now being well brought up country boys we had no idea what a bookie was. We were doing our best to direct a puzzled quartet to MacKay's Bookshop further down High Street when fortunately a more mature and street wise citizen intervened and saved the day. We shot up Stephen's Brae somewhat late for Assembly and eager to tell our classmates about our brief encounter with the Celtic stars."

Exactly half a century later, Inverness would achieve its own team in the SPL and visits to the Highland capital from the likes of Celtic, rare until then, would become commonplace. The twin sources of "Caley All The Way", Alex Main's centenary history of Caledonian FC, and D.J.'s Log Book have enabled me to pinpoint the date of that encounter as Tuesday 5th October 1954. The previous evening, the Monday town holiday, Hugh Grant was among a crowd of over 5000 at Telford Street Park to watch a strong Celtic team go 2-0 up in an exhibition match, only to be pegged back to 2 all. Caley's sensational equaliser came from Malcolm Baillie who a couple of years later would become the father of Heather Baillie, Girl Captain in 1973-74.

As it happens, Hugh and his fellow bus travellers may well have unknowingly passed a bookie's shop every time they traversed Stephen's Brae because by the 60s at any rate, Greenwald's was quarter of the way up on the right. But had Jock Stein and his team mates actually ended up in MacKay's Bookshop, which later became John Menzies and is now W.H. Smith's, they would have had the completely different experience. All that could offer were newspapers, paperbacks and books for sale at the front and the shop's popular MacKay's Library at the back on the right hand side.

Hugh's own football team was Caley, where he served as a member of the management committee, and then Caley Thistle. So although he was a member of Beauly's substantial Roman Catholic community, he never supported Celtic. As one of the Royal Academy's minority of Catholic pupils, he clearly recollects what he calls a regime of "religious apartheid" at the school.

"There would have been about 20 Catholic pupils there in my day, of whom a couple would have been from Beauly and we didn't attend assembly with the rest. Instead we sat separately in the first classroom on D.J.'s right which then looked directly into the hall so we could see the Rector and the first few rows of pupils and hear what he was saying but we weren't actually in what would have been regarded as a Protestant ceremony. It seems so petty now since D.J. would just have a prayer and a hymn. Catholic pupils in these days got no Religious Instruction at all and no chaplain either and I have no recollection of any Roman Catholic priest ever attending the school."

It would seem that into the 60s by the time the new extension opened little had changed, with still separate arrangements for the religious part of assembly at least.

Leo Longmore, nee Leonella Ferrari, joined the staff in September 1961. She was brought up in Inverness and was a member of the Italian family which ran the Ness Café, arguably the source of the best ice cream in town. Leo had been educated at Heatherley private school on Culduthel Road which closed in 1955, two years after she left. Some of its pupils then sat entrance exams for the Academy. She graduated with first class honours in French and Italian from Aberdeen in 1958 and, on her return to Inverness after the new extension opened, has parallel recollections to Hugh Grant's.

"When assembly took place in the hall below I used to sit with the Catholic pupils in Jimmy Johnstone's Room 34 while the Rector would give a hymn and a little homily down below," she recollected. *"Then we would go down and join them for the announcements part of assembly. My brother Renato had been on the staff before I was and he did the same thing. In fact when Renato left to take up a job at the University of Bologna, I was called to see Dr. MacLean the Director of Education and simply offered his job! When I said I wasn't sure if I could do it since I had a very young family, he simply said 'Well just try!' so I did."*

Twenty eight years later in 1989, Leo retired as Principal Teacher of Modern Languages, having succeeded Ellis Stuart in 1973.

These observations are consistent with the log book over a long number of years where references to visits by Catholic clergy are almost non-existent. In stark contrast, over the same lengthy period Protestant ministers, or more specifically those of presbyterian denominations, seemed to be incessantly in and out of the place in a variety of roles. Some visits were for the teaching and examination of religion while other ministers came as school managers, education committee members and exam invigilators.

It may very well seem that the presbyterian churches, even in the third quarter of the 20th century, had a strong foothold in the school. But it would be unwise to make too quick and sweeping a judgement and especially one based on conspiracy, on the lack of input from Catholic clergy. The 1918 Education (Scotland) Act provided for denominational education and led to the setting up of a large number of Catholic schools. Many of these were in west central Scotland but Beauly had its own Catholic primary school and at that time Inverness's St Joseph's catered not only for primary pupils but also had a limited secondary department up to Third Year. As a result it would probably take more research than is possible here to establish the extent to which both sides of the divide were willing partners in this "educational apartheid" at the Royal Academy.

It was not only in the realm of religion that there was a divide at Inverness Royal Academy. There is one question on the sporting side which has always intrigued me. "Was there an institutionalised bias against football and in favour of rugby?" The answer tends to be "It depends on whom you ask."

Ex-rugby players I have discussed this with (and this also tended to be my own experience) often say they never noticed much if anything along these lines. Meanwhile ex-footballers tend to reflect a slightly different view.

Hugh Grant told me: *"I think rugby was slightly more favourably looked upon and I think it was also felt by Frank Cunningham the Geography teacher who ran the football team that rugby players got preference. But there was also shinty and, being a Beauly boy, Curly Stuart who ran that initially welcomed me with open arms. I used to play football for the school team in the morning and then go off to get the Beauly shinty club bus to their game in the afternoon. But when Curly discovered that I wasn't going to be available for the school shinty team because I was playing football, he rather cold shouldered me and didn't speak to me after that."*

In the year behind Hugh Grant and two behind Ian Philip was a sporty girl called Marion Renfrew who left as a Senior Prefect in 1957 to go to study PE.

Mrs Marion Hughes has provided a wide range of anecdotes, including one from her First Year of the event which led to the accession to the throne of Queen Elizabeth II.

"I well remember February 6th, 1952 when the Rector came into our class to tell us that the King had died. Miss Thomson quickly announced that she would have to buy a purple hat for the memorial service to be held later - and she did. She explained to us that purple was a royal colour of mourning.

"Morning Prayers conducted by a very dignified D.J. were another memory. At least once a week either a 1st year boy (either side of D.J.) or 2nd year boy (either side of the stairs) would throw up and Mr Munro the janitor would quickly appear with his bucket of sawdust.

"I don't know if, at the time, we appreciated the amount of time given by staff to extra-curricular activities. Miss Yule took us to hockey matches as far away as Dornoch, Fort William and Aberdeen. Sometimes we did not return till early Saturday evening. I remember one pre-hockey match meeting with Maude P.C. Yule. We felt brave enough to enquire about her forthcoming wedding. 'Oh yes, dearie, I've got a lovely Hoares' hat' - (Hoares was a ladies dress shop in Lombard St.) It is to our credit that we all managed to keep straight faced.

"Frank Cunningham, Janet Banks, Alastair Gammie and many others ran the Outdoor Club which introduced us to the delights of hillwalking. I know that it is an activity that many of us still enjoy to this day - even if it takes a bit longer!

"Exam results did not come via mobile phones, e-mails or even the post. Everybody squeezed into Ethel Forbes' room and D.J. read out each person's results. This was done in alphabetical order for all to hear - a tense wait for those of us towards the end of the alphabet.

"One final memory is of my last day at school when we marched down to the Playhouse Cinema for Prize giving. The choir, conducted by Mr Rogers, sang the Hallelujah Chorus, an ambitious choice, but I can still remember all the words and sing along (out of tune) every time I hear it. I was probably also out of tune in 1957, but being in the choir excused you from lessons!

"The building may have been old and overcrowded, the heating erratic and the toilets outside, but we were taught by a dedicated band of teachers led by an outstanding Rector. Many of us in Inverness, Scotland and beyond have much to be thankful for."

It is more than possible that the Hallelujah Chorus back in the 50s was sung from the same copies of The Messiah as I used myself almost two decades later, given how dog eared ours had by then become.

It is also interesting that Marion's account of prayers in the hall resonates so strongly with that of Brian Denoon who is quoted on the same topic in "Further Up Stephen's Brae".

Log book entry February 1952, including the death of King George VI on the 6th.

251
1952
Feby. 5   In the afternoon the Director of
Education & I interviewed the
three on the leet for the post of
Principal Teacher of Classics,
in succession to Mr McArdle,
who has been appointed to a
similar post in Trinity Academy,
Edinburgh.

" 6   The School Magazine was on
sale this morning.

" "   It was announced to-day
that H.M. King George VI died
peacefully in his sleep last
night. As I did not get the
news officially till just
before lunch-time there was
no time to do anything to-day
but gather the Lower School,
whom Miss Frank addressed.
I also spoke to the pupils in the
Dining Hall.

In the current age of receiving exam results by text, and of data protection and the utmost respect for the confidentiality of the individual, the notion of everybody's results being read out in public seems inconceivable. On the other hand even during my own university days, and for a long time after that, the standard means of announcing results was to post them on a notice board for all to see.

Maude's preferred method of returning class exam results was to put the papers in order and hand them back from the bottom up. That was hard going for the lower achievers and a case of total suspense for the top few, by which time she always seemed to slow down. This was a practice which - with maximum dramatic exploitation - I also copied in my first years in the job but it did seem to become a bit old hat. Latterly it has become more and more common for pupils to ask that their results, even in minor tests, are not read out at all in front of the class.

Colin Fettes, who left in 1970, was the youngest son of the Ardersier G.P. His two older brothers also became doctors and his sister a nurse and this was a family tradition which Colin continued. After studying medicine at Aberdeen he spent the last 29 years of his career as a G.P. in Munlochy on the Black Isle. Now retired from general practice, Colin also made a name for himself in sports medicine and has been international team doctor for Scottish football and shinty squads and for British athletics teams and continues to be a team doctor with the Scottish FA. His biggest moments included the World Athletics championships in Stuttgart in 1993 when his job included accompanying hurdler Colin Jackson for his mandatory post-race drugs test after Jackson had broken the world record. As a souvenir the athlete gave Colin his competitor's logo from the front of his vest which still has a place of honour in the Fettes family home.

Colin Fettes can also take the credit for being one of the very few pupils ever to have had Curly Stuart on the back foot.

"During my time at the Academy I had a very long absence due to illness and when I came back I wasn't quite 100%," he said. *"Then one time in the French class, Curly made me stand up to say something and when I got it wrong I got the usual rap on the side of the head. Between one thing and another I began to feel faint and keeled over and George Chisholm who was sitting behind me thought Curly had killed me or something. So maybe did Curly himself since he seemed to get quite a fright and was terribly apologetic when I came round, which was very unlike him.*

"But Curly was one of quite a few teachers I met after I left who were so much nicer than when we were in school. I also had one or two as patients such as Maude and Jess and even Fritz when I was a student in Aberdeen and it was a pleasure to meet them.

"Coming from out of town I thought I wasn't good enough to play football and had never heard of rugby but was railroaded into playing sports by the tigerish Colin Baillie, for which I remain very grateful (though not so much at the time!) I later discovered he was more of a loveable pussycat! So I ended up playing rugby right through and was eventually prop forward for the First XV.

"I was always so impressed by the walk from the bus station to the school after we arrived in the morning, through First Street and Second Street and the old Falcon Square with these incredibly low doors, roughly where the Eastgate Centre is now. You realised that you were walking through a piece of history and it was in that bit of town that they had filmed that documentary about Culloden a few years earlier where a number of people I knew were extras. I've always been interested in history and Sandy Cameron played a really big part there. He was extremely good at bringing it to life and I still owe Sandy a lot for that. (Very much my own experience as well! - author.)

"One reason I became a doctor was that Jimmy Johnstone, or Abdul as we called him, was the careers teacher and in a very short careers interview he told me that my brothers were studying medicine so maybe I should as well - so I did. And any time I see people doing old fashioned dancing I immediately think of Bill Murray calling out 'away...towards.. step, together, step' as we practised in the gym before school dances. Then there was the Sixth Year boys' common room which the Rector went down to inspect one day and saw something like 'Fatlips is nuts' written on a mirror. He turned to the janitor and said 'Who is this boy Fatlips they keep going on about?' without a clue that this was himself!

"My brother Peter used to fall asleep a bit in class, including Maude's physics lab, so she used him as her definition of inertia. For some reason he was given the job of cutting the grass outside her room on one occasion so she lined up the class to watch him actually doing some work."

*   *   *   *

By any standards, Donald John MacDonald was a remarkable man. Born in Lochcarron in 1900 and educated at Dingwall Academy and Aberdeen University he became the junior member of the English Department at Inverness Royal Academy in 1924. Five years later he was unexpectedly projected into the Principal Teacher's role on the sudden death from pleurisy at the age of just 45 of James Anderson Robertson.

Then when Second Master Alex Duthie retired in 1942, D.J. was further elevated to succeed him, but also remained as P.T. English. It used to be normal for Second Masters (restyled Depute Rectors in the 60s) also to lead a department. Subsequently Donald Graham (1944-50, Gaelic), Leslie "Pop" Frewin (1950-62, Maths) and David Thom (1962-70, Classics) did the same. Then on David Thom's death in post, Jimmy Johnstone, at the time P.T Geography, became W.S. Macdonald's depute and held the post for 19 years.

The rules then changed to restrict any individual to a single promoted post whereupon Robert Preece became head of Geography. This left Jimmy as Depute only, but from 1973 a growing number of Assistant Rectors were also created along with guidance staff and Assistant Principal Teachers when the Houghton agreement substantially increased promoted posts. Just to complete the succession of deputes, Bill Walker followed "JHJ" in 1989, retiring in 2004 by which time assistants had been restyled deputes so the school then had four.

When William Crampton Smith reached the age limit of 65 in January 1944, with the war poised to move into its final and decisive phase, his second in command D.J. MacDonald was ideally placed to succeed him as the 18th Rector of Inverness Royal Academy. However, unlike their deputes, rectors did not lead departments, so the vacancy which brought Fritz in as P.T. English was hence created.

It has already become clear that D.J. MacDonald was universally admired in Inverness and beyond, and prominent among these admirers was Angus MacKenzie.

"The moment we set eyes on D. J. he commanded a huge amount of respect. It was a joy to hear him speaking because his English was so perfect. He didn't teach me personally, but it must have been very inspiring to be in his class and he was such a gentleman. We had school meals over in the Crown School and D.J. would think nothing of sitting down at a table alongside pupils to have his lunch and a chat with them. No one got more Christmas cards than D.J. – he must have had hundreds from pupils.

"And he always had the right quote for the right occasion. For instance at the Installation of Prefects he would quote the Old Testament about Moses appointing able helpers. The message was that he was in charge but the prefects were his helpers. After Buckie retired to Oxfordshire he would come to visit Inverness each year and my wife and I would have Buckie and D.J. over for dinner which always made for a great evening. Buckie of course ran the rugby teams and D.J. was always very supportive, even bringing Mrs MacDonald with him to support school teams when we were playing.

"After he retired and after he moved from Kenneth Street up to Green Drive, he contacted me one day – this would have been in the late 60s – and asked me if I would look after his business affairs. He said he was fed up writing cheques and dealing with bills and he wanted me to do all

of that for him including a mandate to sign cheques. I just felt so honoured that he should ask me to do something like that for him."

As an individual D. J. MacDonald has fascinated me for decades, although to some extent I see two sides to him. My earliest memory is of this rather small, grey, bald and much venerated elderly gentleman who would pop up from time to time for major school functions when I was a pupil. I have slightly mixed feelings about that because the mark he left on the school was so profound that, after he retired in January 1962, he was an incredibly hard act for W. S. to follow. As such it might have been better if he had stayed away just a little more and allowed things to move on but the school always seemed to want him back. At this point I am going to attempt to look inside the head of D. J. MacDonald.

On the first day of summer term on April 17th 1961, his log book records (note the use of the third person singular): *"At prayers the Rector thanked the school for their sympathy on the death of his wife on April 5, and for the beautiful wreath sent to her funeral."* Clearly Mrs MacDonald had died during the Easter holidays.

Then on August 23rd, the first day of the following term: *"Session 1961-62 commenced. During the holidays the resignation of the Rector, Dr D.J. MacDonald, was announced. He retires on Friday 12th January 1962."*

The timing here is interesting and seems to have been well thought out. The period between his summer holiday resignation notice and January departure seems just long enough for a successor to be identified and then to serve three months' notice with his existing employer. On October 11th, presumably following the interviews, D. J. reveals that his successor will be *"Mr Wm Macdonald MBE, DSC, MA, BA* (he seems to have omitted the Dip Ed!), *Rector of Campbeltown Grammar School."* He also reveals that W.S. would take up his post on Monday January 15th 1962, almost exactly three months later and the Monday after his own departure which had been worked out all these weeks previously.

This is all completely consistent with the view I have frequently heard that D.J. was hit hard by his wife's death at a relatively early age. It is not clear what her health had been like before that, but five years previously, D.J. did record his absence to take her for an electrocardiogram. Angus MacKenzie also reinforced my view as to how close they were. As a result, at 61, he felt unable to continue in post for much longer, even though retirement at 65 would then have been normal. It would seem that by the time he got to the end of the session he just decided to call it a day and resigned over the holidays. But at the same time – typically of the man – he did the decent thing and gave the Education Authority long enough to appoint a successor and achieve a seamless join, although only just.

However, I think I also detect mixed feelings. Although he may not have felt able to sustain the full rigours of leading the school, I also believe that he felt reluctant to let go entirely and hence readily accepted opportunities for cameo reappearances. Indeed these went on until 1978 when he performed the official opening of the Culduthel building (Chapter 5), and I have recollections of his presence at stage shows even after that.

The possible down side of that was that his successor, who even shared the same surname, may have felt just a bit overshadowed by the educational colossus and local legend whose intermittent reappearances continued. On the other hand we have no way of knowing on whose initiative these took place, given the regard in which he was held.

Many former pupils speak of D.J.'s "presence" and this is a vital ingredient of the man who led the school for exactly 18 years. There is absolutely no doubt that he did a very good job, initially in difficult times of war and then extreme austerity, although the largely well-heeled clientele of Inverness Royal Academy may have been better insulated from the latter than most. He was also hugely well regarded in the community, as illustrated by the external posts he held such as on the Hospitals Board, the Inverness Presbytery of the Church of Scotland and as a J.P. His own former University, Aberdeen, honoured him in 1957 by creating him an honorary Ll.D. – Doctor of Laws - after which he was publicly elevated from plain "Mr" to "Dr D.J. MacDonald".

He was also a member of the Rotary Club in an era when that body regarded itself as much more exclusive than it does today. He punctiliously recorded in the Log, on his appointment that he would be late arriving back in school on Thursday afternoons following the Rotary lunch.

However, this was the mere tip of the iceberg since the log is also full of references to his absences on the business of various organisations which had nothing to do with education, such as those mentioned above. This is not atypical of the era since Bill Murray and Janet Banks took regular forays to meetings of the Scottish Country Dance Society while David Thom was a frequent absentee on Boys' Brigade business and various Gaelic teachers adjudicated at local and national mods.

However, I think there is a little more to D.J.'s enormous status both in education and the community than his substantial personal merit, and it goes back to the earlier concept of "presence". This was a man of strong religious faith and with a powerful blend of abilities. I also believe that people's perception of these abilities, and hence the regard in which he was held, were further enhanced by his extremely compelling personality. In other words he had charisma and exploited it quite substantially.

However, there was maybe also just a bit of transparency and possibly even pretension from time to time. This did become apparent to a certain cynical young teacher in the 70s when D.J. was guest speaker at a St Columba High Church AGM I attended. Here I found him coming away, not for the first, with one liners like "You will remember what Gibbon said in his 'Decline and Fall of the Roman Empire'......".

Now to be realistic, the "You will remember...." bit was just a bit superior and pretentious, because he knew quite well that nobody did. But I did at the time also wonder if he was just chancing his arm completely over his knowledge of the work in question. Then over 30 years later, that scepticism was finally put to bed when I visited Angus MacKenzie to interview him for this book and he showed me D.J.'s leather bound set of Gibbon's work which the former rector had given him.

In the dying days of 1985, as a rookie BBC journalist, I visited him in his apartment at Abbeyfield Home. What I recorded was the 85 year old relating with crystal clarity his memories of New Year as a youngster in Lochcarron before the First World War. I was also highly gratified on that occasion at the kind words he had about my performance for the Academy in Television Top Of The Form quiz 15 years previously

Morning Interval in the hall – early 1950's

where he had been in the audience for a number of our recordings. That possibly reflected one of his greatest talents as a school leader - making people feel valued.

Whilst researching "Further Up Stephen's Brae" in the late 1990s I first delved into the school log books. Now at this point I find myself in danger of being as literarily pretentious as D.J. himself, since I need to quote John Keats' sonnet "On first looking into Chapman's Homer".

The poet was overawed by his first insight into this translation of the Greek giant's works. In similar vein I was also equally impressed on my first inspection of D.J. MacDonald's 18 years of contributions to the Inverness Royal Academy log book. What he has to say and what he reveals about school life just seem to get better and better as this tenure goes by. So, remembering the colour of the prefects' braid, Keats' opening iambic pentameter - "Much have I travell'd in the realms of gold" - would appear to apply extremely well.

"On first looking into D.J's Log Book" impressed me hugely then and has done so ever since.

In stark contrast, Crampton Smith's entries from 1920-44 are relatively sterile and functional and for "Further Up Stephen's Brae" I probably extracted as much as is realistic. Similarly Willie Fatlips was a very nice man, ran a really good school and in terms of his credentials – even with the Dip Ed omitted! - actually vastly outshone D.J. in whose shadow he lingered excessively. W.S. had honours degrees in different subjects from two universities. He had an enviable naval war record which included captaining a corvette and the interrogation of German POW. He also had sufficient expertise to teach his pupils Navigation as well as French and German. Then there was his status as an amateur international footballer.

But he seems to have viewed the school log in an entirely different light from his predecessor and during his tenure it reverts to a far more functional - and much less legible - account of the administrative trivia of the school.

In total contrast D.J.'s contributions convey a vivid 18 year picture - a movie even, and in full technicolour - of what life was like at Inverness Royal Academy when he was in charge.

The product has therefore been just too tempting to miss. D.J.'s log book entries were central to the previous chapter on session 1958-59 but there are so many others which are so illuminating that the best of them just have to be detailed here.

Such are their atmospheric qualities that my extensive examination of them has created a vivid mind picture of what the school was like in the 50s in particular. The clarity of that picture was brought home when I came across a remarkable 10 minute silent cine film of the 1952 school sports taken by Jimmy Nairn of Caledonian Associated Cinemas. Some of those in it, such as Bill Murray, David Thom, and Kate MacLean, I had known personally and eventually taught me. But as I watched, others simply sprang from the screen at me as characters from the pages of D.J.'s log books and school magazines. With the background of the log books, between one thing and another I felt as if I was really there.

The film, which also brilliantly conveys a flavour of what school sports were like at the old field for very many years, can be found at **http://ssa.nls.uk/film.cfm?fid=0626**.

Even by the 1950s, school discipline had softened just a bit compared with the turn of the century when W.J. Watson would record in his log, in red, sanctions such as "16 lashes" or "8 lashes and a warning" for truancy. The infrequency of references to corporal punishment by the post war years certainly does not suggest that it had by any means disappeared. But by the 50s an edict was issued that pupils were not to be hit on the head (Curly must have been absent that day!) and that girls were not to be strapped.

One rare record comes on 13th October 1960 when a Third Year boy *"defied the authority of Mr. Murdo MacKay, teacher of Gaelic, during a period of private study and refused to take punishment. I ordered him to take it and he did. In my presence Mr. MacKay gave him four strokes of the strap."*

"Refusing the belt" was regarded as pretty serious at the time, but sometimes the Lochgelly was administered even when the teacher had got things wrong. These is a tale - possibly Apocryphal - that a pupil once arrived at W.S. Macdonald's room with the words "Mr X sent me down....." and was promptly belted. It was only when that was complete that the hapless pupil continued "But sir, he only sent me down with this note for you!"

In "Further up Stephen's Brae" I related how two pupils had placed a bogus advert for a janitor in The Courier, bringing 70 men to the school. The boys had come close to expulsion but instead had been "arraigned" at assembly. Just over a fortnight later the older of the two, a Sixth Year pupil, had been caught truanting and was instantly expelled.

Public humiliation like this in front of the school seems to have been a particular tactic of D.J. In 1960, two culprits were found to have damaged plaster in the boys' toilet and *"they were seen about it and pilloried at morning assembly."*

D.J.had a very acute sense of the school's status within the community and also of the community's perception of it. As always, image needed to match substance and what the public thought of Inverness Royal Academy was very important to him. I would have loved to have worked with him as school PR officer!

Inverness Royal Academy
SESSION 1963-1964

RECTOR
WILLIAM S. MACDONALD, M.B.E., D.S.C., M.A., Dip.Ed., B.A.

Second Master
DAVID THOM, M.A.

Lady Superintendent
Miss ETHEL C. FORBES, M.A.

Classics
DAVID THOM, M.A., Hons. in Classics (Glas.).
Miss JESSIE E. THOMSON, M.A., Hons. in Classics (Edin.).
Mrs CATHERINE J. MACDONALD, M.A. (Aberd.).
Miss JEAN M. OSLER, M.A., Hons. in Classics (Edin.).

English
JACOB H. MOWAT, M.A., Hons. in English (Edin.).
JAMES E. H. HUTCHEON, M.A., Hons. in English (Aberd.).
ALAN MACGILLIVRAY, M.A., Hons. in English, Dip.Ed. (Edin.).
ALAN J. DOUGHERTY, M.A., Hons. in English (Aberd.).
J. DOUGLAS KENNEDY, M.A., Hons. in English (Aberd.).
Mrs LELIA G. HOLM, M.A. (Aberd.).
Miss JANE E. D. THOMS, M.A., Hons. in English (St Andrews).

History
ALEXANDER D. CAMERON, M.A., Hons. in History, Dip.Ed. (Edin.).
Miss BARBARA C. SPENCE, M.A., Hons. in History (Glas.).

Geography
JAMES H. JOHNSTONE, M.A., Hons. in Geography (Aberd.).
JAMES McINTOSH, B.Sc., Hons. in Geography (Aberd.).
Miss ANNIE M. SKINNER, M.A. (Aberd.).

French and Italian
WILLIAM E. STUART, M.A., Hons. in French and Italian (Edin.).
Miss CHRISTINE D. FORBES, B.A. (Oxon.), L.R.A.M.
Miss JANET K. DOUGLAS, M.A. (Edin.).
Miss SHEENA H. LANCASTER, M.A. (Aberd.).
IAN TORQUIL MACLEOD, M.A., Hons. in French and Latin (Aberd.).
Mrs LEONELLA L. LONGMORE, M.A., Hons. in French and Italian (Aberd.).
Miss PATRICIA A. BARNARD, M.A. (Edin.).
M. JEAN COUSQUER, Student Assistant.

German
Miss MARY I. CLARK, M.A., Hons. in German (Edin.).

Music
NINIAN J. S. BOWMAN, A.R.C.M.
DAVID C. McINTOSH, M.A., B.Mus. (Glas.).

Art
JOHN S. D. JOHNSTON, D.A., Post-Graduate (Edin.).
CHARLES J. BUCHANAN, D.A. (Drawing and Painting) (Glas.).
GORDON L. HARVEY, D.A. (Design) (Aberd.).

Mathematics

ALLAN S. WILSON, B.Sc. (Glas.), Hons. in Mathematics and Natural Philosophy.

Miss JANET BANKS, M.A. (Aberd.), Hons. in Mathematics and Natural Philosophy.

Miss ETHEL C. FORBES, M.A. (Edin.).

Miss PATRICIA R. FORBES, M.A. (Aberd.).

Mrs ANNICE D. HARDIE, M.A. (Edin.), Hons. in Mathematics and Natural Philosophy.

MURDO J. MACDONALD, B.Sc. (Glas.).

Gaelic

LACHLAN G. DICK, M.A. (Glasgow).

Science

THOMAS FRASER, B.Sc. (Aberd.), Hons. in Chemistry, F.E.I.S.

Dr CHARLES E. STEWART, B.Sc., Hons. in Physical Chemistry ; Ph.D. (Glas.), Physical Research (Aldermaston).

ROBERT WRIGHT, B.Sc. (Leeds), Hons. in Botany, Dip.Ed., F.L.S.

Mrs MAUDE P. C. ANDERSON, B.Sc. (St Andrews), Hons. in Physics.

HUGH W. MACDONALD, B.Sc. (Glas.).

PETER R. HIGGINS, B.Sc. (Edin.), Hons. in Chemistry.

JOHN W. CAMPBELL, B.Sc. (Glas.).

ALLAN C. BARCLAY, B.Sc. (Glas.), Hons. in Physics.

Needlework

Miss JANET A. ROSE, Group I Diploma of College of Domestic Science, Edinburgh.

Technical Subjects

ALEXANDER A. BEATTIE, (National Certificate in Mechanical Engineering).

Physical Education

WILLIAM MURRAY, Diploma of Scottish School of Physical Education and Hygiene.

COLIN A. D. BAILLIE, Diploma of Scottish School of Physical Education and Hygiene (part time).

Miss ALISON B. M. BUCHAN, Diploma of Dunfermline College of Physical Education, Aberdeen.

Careers Master

JAMES H. JOHNSTONE, M.A.

Warden of Drummond Park Boys' Hostel

MALCOLM CUMMING, B.Sc.

Warden of Hedgefield Girls' Hostel

Miss ELIZABETH CAMPBELL, B.E.M.

RECTOR'S SECRETARY — Miss MARY B. McGILL

ASSISTANT SECRETARY — Mrs CATHERINE K. STEWART

JANITOR — Mr ALEXANDER MUNRO   GROUNDSMAN — Mr JOHN MURDOCH

ASSISTANT JANITOR — Mr DANIEL MACKENZIE

When he needed to be firm with parents he was, and on at least one occasion there was a prosecution for persistent truancy. Then there was the implied disapproval after the 1960 Installation of Prefects where he records that *"the parents of all prefects but one turned up"*.

So does this suggest the out and out expectation that parents would just turn up en masse of a midweek afternoon, on the assumption that they could and should simply be able to abandon their employment at the drop of a hat?

If, for instance, some father had phoned up D.J. to say that he had a G.P. surgery to take, an audit to perform or legal business to transact on behalf of a client, might such an approach have elicited a rapid change of tune? Or indeed if Miss Young had been Mrs Young!?

But then if the parent had a train to drive to Wick or a gas cooker to install, would the response have been the same? On the other hand I'm not sure how many progeny of train drivers or gas fitters became Royal Academy prefects in these days!

The school did have its fair share of difficult parents. One during the 50s contested the school nurse's decision to send his children home with suspected impetigo. Then by session 1960-61, with the primary department down to just P7, three mothers *"....complained of 1 - Fees being charged now that the children are in Crown School annexe. 2 - That the roof is leaking. 3 - That the heating is inadequate. 4 - That there are no pegs on which to hang coats. The Rector reported the conversation to Mr. Lawson, Depute Director of Education."*

That last sentence is in itself intriguing because Mr. Lawson would also then have been a fee-paying parent of a P7 pupil. His daughter Janet was a member of that very last P7 class. She left S6 in 1967 with some interesting school magazine reflections on her early pupil years which are on page 96 of "Further Up Stephen's Brae". Here she asked the incontestable question as to how she could be reprimanded for not having her eyes closed during a prayer at assembly since the teacher concerned was presumably not in a position to be able to make the necessary observation?

Apart from some parents, D.J. also sometimes had difficulties with staff. In the case of teaching staff, concerns are very occasional, implied and even obscurely stated. In one or two instances, difficulties with non-teaching staff are more specifically expressed, such as during his early days in post when he makes periodic references to problems with a janitor. Over a period of about four years the situation appears steadily to have deteriorated through phases of warnings and eventual dismissal for "neglect of duty". Then eviction from the janitor's house also had to be threatened but the place was eventually vacated for renovations to be completed for its next occupant Alec Munro who held the post for 24 years until 1972.

Before his dismissal, that same janitor was also a victim. In September 1946 he was *".....absent in the Infirmary suffering from what may be a broken nose. He reports that a Pole, unprovoked, attacked him in Eastgate at 10:30pm on Saturday."*

The Rector goes on to relate in the same entry how a female member of staff *".....was assaulted by some man at present unidentified on Saturday night in Broadstone Park."* Two days later the woman was *"...absent from school in the forenoon to attend identification parade at the Barracks."*

It is not revealed whether this was the same man who had simply gone on the rampage. It's also worth asking whether in the current era his nationality would receive highlight?

Then there was the case of the groundsman who was invited to resign, and did, after being discovered working in a filling station when he was being paid to look after the school field.

There was also an instance where a Second Year pupil was caught stealing from pockets in the cloakrooms. Not for the first time, the tone of D.J.'s references to the performance of an illegal or dishonest act has a strange moral resonance with the tone of some of Enid Blyton's books which I read extensively as a child. In particular it resonates with "Six Bad Boys", a tale of juvenile delinquency which, as a primary pupil, I found mildly disturbing. A lot of Blyton's works were, of course, contemporary with D.J.'s tenure so maybe this is simply a reflection of the perceptions and values of the period.

The autumn of 1954 seems to have seen problems with the heating system due to the fuel used.

"We began burning Brora ovoids in the furnaces and staff room fires. The first noticeable reaction from the former is heavy smoke." For many years there had been an active coalfield in Sutherland, but this does not appear to have been a very successful attempt to patronise it.

Valentine's Day 1955 sees a somewhat enigmatic entry which reads: *"Dr MacLean, Director of Education, and Mr. Lawson, Dep. Director, spent Saturday forenoon in the school studying accommodation in view of the coming increase in world population."*

By the mid-50s it had become all too clear that a post-war Baby Boom was well underway and these youngsters would soon require secondary education. It could therefore be inferred that this visit may have initiated two developments which would have a profound impact on the school. Firstly, on June 30th 1955 it emerges that: *"The Education Committee at their June meeting decided to discontinue the Primary Department by stopping intake now in order to make room for the growth of the Secondary Department."*

This must have been something of a cliffhanger of a decision because here is an announcement on the very last day of one session that there would be no P1 class at the start of the next in just eight weeks' time. Apart from the decision's unpopularity within the school, one has to wonder how controversial this all was, with council debate perhaps continuing until the very last day before a ruling was made. As a result, a question also arises as to whether the final closure of the primary department in 1961, which occurred across the same holidays as D.J. decided to resign, may have been an additional minor factor there?

Then the second development which may have originated from this 1955 investigation into school capacity was very possibly the new extension on which work began just three years later. That is also something which, by the summer of 1961, was also well and truly complete.

So by the time that summer came round, with his dear wife gone, but also the Primary department finally closed and the school building complete, extended and renovated, maybe the 18th Rector of Inverness Royal Academy saw this as a time to make a break. We will never know for certain. On January 12th 1962, after almost 38 years at the school, 18 of them at the helm - and his magnificent log book entries - come to an end with this simple statement:

4 - LATTER DAYS AT THE TOP OF THE BRAE – THE 1970s

In the summer of 1975 I left Edinburgh University with £27 for the class prize in Chemistry, an honours degree certificate with "summa cum laude" on it and a reputation as a firebug! Four years at Edinburgh had also included courses as diverse as Physics, Maths, History of Science and even Business Studies. But these were all subsidiary to my main degree subject of Chemistry which I pursued for the entire duration of my stay.

During my final year research project I had been drying the flammable hydrocarbon toluene with sodium metal and contrived to get quite a lot of both down my sink where they inevitably met water. The resulting reaction sparked off a conflagration which forced the emergency evacuation of the entire lab and the incineration of the immediate area. This was a rather inauspicious start to a project which was eventually published in the Journal of the Chemical Society and it did perhaps suggest that practical Chemistry was not one of my strong points.

The incident was still completely unrelated to my decision not to pursue further research through a PhD. That had already been made a year previously and instead I had opted for a one year post graduate teaching qualification at Aberdeen College of Education. The reasons for choosing teaching over my original PhD plan are complex. Apart from an enthusiasm for the job itself, there was an eye for the main chance of working back home in Inverness as well as holidays and conditions of service which would allow me to become involved in various other interests, including coaching athletics.

My year in Aberdeen yielded teaching qualifications in Chemistry and Science - and in Maths which was very much a third option. But at a time of severe Maths teacher shortage, I thought this might make me rather more employable - and ultimately it did.

Before I went to Aberdeen that September, I had to do a fortnight's pre-college observation in a school, and Inverness Royal Academy was the obvious and indeed the only choice. This proved to be a turning point because the very first Monday morning I walked back into these familiar and much loved surroundings, I was greeted in Room 19 by a very flustered Jim Dunlop. He had taken over as Principal Teacher of Chemistry in 1973 when Jim Sim had become one of these new-fangled Assistant Rectors.

Jim Sim's promotion was a result of the Houghton pay deal of the early 70s which included the new management posts of Assistant Rector and also Principal and Assistant Principal Teachers of Guidance. The original Assistant Rectors had been Bill Murray, whose "leisure" remit effectively gave him official recognition for the plethora of administrative jobs he had done for years, and Sandy Cameron who had a curricular role. Sandy left after only a short tenure and Jim Sim succeeded him. Meanwhile the school's first two Principal Teachers of Guidance, looking after pupils' educational, pastoral and moral welfare, were Margaret Murray and Torquil MacLeod.

Here I was returning to a somewhat changed school environment to partake of what should have involved nothing more than sitting in the back of a class for a fortnight, watching the job being done by qualified professionals. However, Margaret Murray, who had occupied Room 17 at the bottom of the art stairs since Pete Higgins had left in the late 60s, was off ill and was likely to be absent for some time. So Jim Dunlop wondered if I would mind solving his staffing crisis by taking Margaret's classes for the fortnight? Simple as that!

With not the slightest notion of the enormity of what I was taking on, I simply said "Well OK then". And that was it. Twenty minutes later, with not an iota of preparation, I was standing on the dais in Room 19 from which I had myself been taught Higher and Sixth Year studies, imparting the basics of chemical bonding to a Fifth Year starter "O" Grade class.

This would never have been allowed in the current era, but it was the best thing that ever happened to me. It simply let me get on with the job I wanted to learn, albeit with the safeguard of only having generally well mannered, largely academic pupils to deal with. I started off with something like a Higher, Third and Fourth Year "O" Grades and that starter class - not a particularly heavy timetable as it happens, due to Margaret's reduced teaching load with her guidance commitment.

So what was life like in Inverness in that late summer of 1975 when I first stood at the business end of a classroom? In the wider world, the Suez Canal reopened for the first time after the Yom Kippur war of October 73, the Government took control of British Leyland Motors and Gerald Ford, who succeeded Richard Nixon in the White House post-Watergate, survived two assassination attempts.

For Saturday night entertainment in the capital of the Highlands there was the Caledonian Hotel where organisations like Culduthel Badminton Club could earn funds by sponsoring a late licence. This would allow drinking on a dance or disco night after the still standard pub closing time of 10pm. With 11pm closing not far away, there would soon be also competition from those legendary discos at Highland Rugby Club over at the Canal Field.

Compared with modern day night clubs, late openings – even subject to recent controversial midnight curfews – what was on offer in Inverness in the mid 70s waspretty basic. But on the other hand, as in so many other areas of life, expectations were also correspondingly lower in an era of rather lower sophistication.

Fort Augustus outdoor centre.

DO-IT-YOURSELF OUTDOOR CENTRE

The Education Committee has generously made available the old Fort Augustus School for development as an Academy Outdoor Centre. The possession of such a Centre adds a new dimension to the life of a school. New things become possible and established activities are more readily pursued. Would you agree it might work in the following way?

PHYSICAL/RECREATIONAL ACTIVITIES
Walking, climbing, orienteering, sailing, canoeing, fishing.

FIELD STUDIES and STUDY GROUPS
Map-reading, geography, geology, weather, history, archaeology, zoology, art and drama 'Workshops.'

SOCIAL ACTIVITIES
Cookery, ceilidhs, barbecues, conservation projects, community service in local village, organisation and allocation of routine duties.

BENEFIT TO PUPILS
Enjoyment.
Good health.
Development of leisure interests.
A realisation that other people matter.
Development of happy and creative relationships.
Interest and realism added to school subjects.

We now have the building; the rest remains to do. We must consult, plan and set priorities; we must raise money and spend money; we must sweep, scrub, paint and modify; eventually we must devise programmes of activities. It is a project which will require enthusiasm, imagination and a conviction that it is very much worthwhile. It is something we can tackle together. There is a Staff Outdoor Centre Development Committee: why not a Pupils' Committee?

20

During my initial fortnight "back up Stephen's Brae", the programme at the La Scala – now Inverness's only purpose built cinema since the arson attack on the Playhouse in 1972 – included Mel Brooks' "Young Frankenstein" and "The Sting" with Paul Newman and Robert Redford. There was also The Little Theatre, part of the Arts Centre in Farraline Park in the old Bell's School building.

That seated around 100 and was all Inverness had in those years between the closure of the Empire Theatre and the opening of Eden Court. It was showing "The Massacre Of Glencoe" starring James Robertson Justice, better known as Sir Lancelot Spratt in the "Doctor" films. Admission was 70p, or 40p for children. Alternatively in the Cummings Hotel there were The Corries complete with white Aran jumpers. Top of the Record Rendezvous charts was Rod Stewart's "Sailing" which is as good an example as I have ever heard of how not to sing.

Fraserburgh got off to a flying start in the Highland League, only to be overhauled after the first fortnight by Caley. However that season's title would eventually become Nairn County's first. In an era before the

Inverness rivalry which Caley and Thistle had before their 1994 merger, Caley and Clach were going through an especially acrimonious phase.

An Inverness Courier headline in September 1975 reminds me of Inverness District Council's historic inability to come to a decision on football related matters. Almost 20 years later the District Council would dither and dither about Caley's proposed relocation to the Carse and later about whether or not to give Caley Thistle £900,000 - a decision it never ultimately made. So it was in anticipation of a lot more of the same that in 1975 the paper trumpeted "No Decision on Caley's Plans". On the other hand, with only adverts on the front and a Victorian single column layout on the news pages, the Inverness Courier in these days didn't really "trumpet" very loudly at all.

In 1975 the burning football issue was Caley wanting to erect floodlights at a training area which was apparently too near the Merkinch for Clach to be comfortable with the plan. So they lodged a counter proposal, presumably to their neighbours' great annoyance.

Then it was announced that Clach would be raising the Highland League flag they had won the previous season at their next home game. This was very far into the season for such a ceremony. But the delay may just have had something to do with the opposition at Grant Street that day being Caley, and Clach wanting to celebrate right in the faces of their local rivals!

Later that September I was back in Inverness for my first formal teaching practice of four weeks at the High School. In the interim, I had spent a short time at the College in Aberdeen and immediately ditched my plans to incorporate a Dip. Ed. into my studies. I had quickly concluded that I really wasn't all that keen on the theoretical educational guff that would be involved. I just wanted to get on with teaching.

Arriving at the High School was a revelation because this was the first time I had ever set foot inside a comprehensive school. After six years of highly selective education at the top of the hill followed by four years at Edinburgh University, it was time to see how the other three quarters lived. Suffice it to say that this showed me a lot and it did help me adapt quite quickly to an approach to teaching completely different from what I had seen in my own youth. This spell at the High School was also where I first met Morton Roer with whom I would forge a close 30 year professional association when he came up to Culduthel in 1978, eventually becoming Principal Teacher on Jim Dunlop's retiral in 1994.

Then the following February, after what felt like a mind numbing infinity of theoretical lectures on educational topics at Aberdeen College, I returned at my own request for my next practice to Inverness Royal Academy. Margaret was off once more so I simply got my September timetable back again. I think Jim had decided that I had done well enough first time round so they just let me get on with it, for which I was eternally grateful.

1976 Prefects and Obituaries including the legendary Fritz.

PREFECTS

Back row: John Kay, Neil Walker, Suzanne Ross, Alison Wray, Rachel Cartilage, Fiona Macmillan, Elaine MacGruer.
Middle row: Eric Fraser, Fiona MacIntosh, Archie Campbell, Elizabeth Snape, Tom MacIntyre, Carol Kelly, George Gunn, Gillian Stewart, Alastair Sim.
Front row: Callum Mackintosh, Patricia Farquharson (vice-captain), Miss Rose, Roddy Innes (captain), The Rector, Rose Rollo (captain), Mr Johnstone, Jean-Pierre Sieczkarek (vice-captain), Ruth Handford.

OBITUARIES

MR J. H. MOWAT

It was with very deep regret that we heard, just as we were going to press, of the death on the 22nd May of Mr J. H. Mowat, who retired as Head of the English Department in 1968.

MRS CATHERINE K. STEWART

Mrs Cathie Stewart, who gave fourteen years of valuable service to the Academy, died on the 21st January, 1975. Mrs Stewart joined the office staff as a part-time clerical assistant in 1960 and took over the post of Rector's Secretary in 1969. Invariably helpful and obliging to staff and pupils, Mrs Stewart is remembered in the Academy with gratitude and affection.

MRS ANNICE D. HARDIE

It was with deep regret that we heard of the death on the 19th December of Mrs Annice Hardie, who taught mathematics here in the Academy from 1956 until she retired in 1971. Mrs Hardie's ready wit enlivened both class-room and staff-room, and the cheerful courage with which she bore a burden of increasingly poor health was admired by all who knew her. She will be greatly missed by her family, former colleagues and many friends.

These experiences worked wonders in preparing me for the real job at a time when I was also less than impressed by the wooly minded theorists, some with limited classroom experience, in Aberdeen who lectured on obscure aspects of education and psychology which really didn't appeal to me at all. In fact being twice cast straight in at the deep end, aged 22, in front of a class at Inverness Royal Academy probably did quite a lot to formulate what is a pretty uncomplicated approach to the job of teaching.

My aversion to all this educational theory certainly helps to explain why, once in the job, applying for a promoted post never really appealed to me and I decided instead to pursue parallel careers in broadcasting and journalism. But at least that could then turn full circle when I became able to use these other skills in the Senior Teacher's post which I got in 1995. That had nothing whatsoever to do with educational theory but allowed me to use my other skills and contacts and get on with being the school's press officer and newsletter editor.

What I returned to in February 1976 was a Midmills building which, apart from a new block in the back car park housing Biology, Business Studies and a bit more, was essentially the same as when I had left as a pupil almost five years previously. But the educational mix had changed quite markedly. Of the pupils, only the Sixth Year - who had been in S1 when I was in S6 so were the only ones still there - had had to sit the Promotion exam to get into Inverness Royal Academy. S3, 4 and 5 had all done their first two years at Millburn as part of the start of a complex transition towards comprehensive education in Inverness.

It was only some years later that Eddie Hutcheon explained to me that, while I had been away at university, there had been real fears that this process might also involve the complete closure of the Royal Academy. However, in the face of quite widespread opposition, this danger had been averted.

This transitional arrangement was why the Royal Academy now had no S1 or S2 because now it was fed from Millburn in S3 by those deemed capable of doing at least one Higher. As a result there was a significant change in intake since the entry level was rather lower than it had been in the Promotion days. It also included the high fliers only from the east side of the River Ness since everyone from the west in the mid-70s went to the High School. In addition the lack of S1 and S2 and the absence of their passionate high pitched enthusiasm was certainly noticeable compared with what I had known a few years previously as a pupil. But despite that, I have to say that the fundamental tone of the school wasn't greatly different when I came back as a student and a lot of the traditions, values and practices were more or less unchanged.

One member of staff who arrived in the early months of this transition was Bill Walker who was appointed Principal Teacher of Physics in February 1972 on the departure of Jim Wilson.

Originally from Fraserburgh, Bill became PT Physics in February 1972 on the departure of Jim Wilson. He had already taught for just over four years at Aberdeen Grammar School and a further seven years on was promoted to Assistant Rector to replace Derek McGinn on his departure to Culloden Academy. Then in 1990 Bill succeeded Jimmy Johnstone to the Depute Rector's office across the corridor, and retired in 2004. One particular feature of the old school struck him very quickly indeed.

"One thing I would always associate Midmills with was the camaraderie among the staff which was amazingly good," he said. *"Midmills was the kind of place that a lot of people came to and either stayed there for the rest of their careers or only otherwise left through promotion. That camaraderie never came back again up at Culduthel and I think one of the reasons was the layout of the building with separate staff bases which didn't help. One regular feature of Midmills was the gathering every Friday after school in the Kingsmills Hotel for afternoon tea. It had been the Playhouse before early 1972 when the cinema was destroyed by fire just three weeks after I arrived in Inverness. In fact that night I was heading there from the Crown where I lived at the time to see the film 'Le Mans' but when I got there it was well alight so I just had to go home again.*

"The first staff presentation I attended was Jess Thomson's in the summer of 1972 at the Meallmore Lodge Hotel on the old A9. It was a lunch which started at 2pm and Jess started speaking at 4 - for a whole hour but it felt like just 10 minutes because she was so hilarious. She had a whole lot of Latin quotes, some of them genuine, others just made up, and it was brilliant. That was an extremely jovial occasion.

"At Midmills it was just S3-6 and largely academic in nature. At one point there were seven Higher Physics classes in the department and a Sixth Year studies class of 32. During my entire teaching career I would say I came across about five pupils of outstanding academic ability, some of them at Aberdeen Grammar, but Bruce MacPherson who was dux of the Royal Academy in 1976 would certainly have been among them. But I also joined a happy band of Janet Banks, Patsy Forbes, Alan Findlay, Andrew Fraser and a few others during what was a fantastic period with the Outdoor Club in the 70/80s. Pupil members included people like Jock Ramsay and Alan Barrie and I remember on one occasion whilst coming back down Ben Nevis, Jock's body started moving faster than his legs and he went straight into a boulder the size of a house. We had to take him to hospital and fortunately he wasn't seriously hurt. Despite medical

advice otherwise, he was playing rugby the following weekend, sustaining further injury!"

With the less stringent criteria for entry through Millburn, there were certainly a lot more academic strugglers in classes. But by now they had guidance teachers to help orientate them in the right direction. And as Bill confirms, there were still huge numbers of presentations at "O" Grade, Higher and Sixth Year Studies. One change in S4 was that the straight pass or fail at "O" Grade was replaced by A, B and C in 1973.

There had certainly been changes among the staff, with stalwarts like Jess, Curly, Hairy Hugh, Sandy Cameron and indeed Willie Fatlips himself all gone in these intervening years. But long term players like Eddie Hutcheon, Allan Wilson, Maude, Jimmy Johnstone and especially that archetypal guardian of Inverness Royal Academy tradition Bill Murray were still in post in the early years of Ian Fraser's rectorship. Bill had played a central role at the school since his arrival in 1951 and the introduction of sports colours had been just one of his several innovations. He also created the physical age group system for the school sports and developed the house system into a fine art.

No former pupil can ever forget the blue, green, red and yellow house flags set out in alphabetical order for Abertarff, Dunain, Farr and Raigmore when it came to sports day. Bill's school sports were one of the jewels in the crown of athletics in the north for their precision of organisation and this was something he also translated into rugby and everything else he did. I say these things very much as one of "Bill's Boys" for most of my six years as a pupil.

Although Bill left in 1977, enough of the "old school" remained on the premises for a lot of the traditions to be maintained in an era of evolution from selective to comprehensive education.

MR. WILLIAM MURRAY

That is also borne out by a look through school magazines of the mid 70s where there is little evidence of much change since the previous decade - apart from the fashions. By the time I left in 1971 things had begun to change despite the most vigorous of rearguard actions, especially against lengthening hair among the boys, by W. S. Macdonald. Ian Fraser may have had a more liberal view, or social pressures may simply have become too strong to resist. But just half a decade later Inverness Royal Academy was well into male perms, flares, big collars and all the other sartorial embarrassments which made the 70s unique.

1975

Mrs McIntyre and our Senior Choir.

Extra-curricular activities continued to flourish and the 1975 photo of the school choir shows 50 pupils along with Anne MacIntyre who had taken over as Principal Teacher of Music after Ian Bowman had left for Wick a couple of years previously. This was also in the warm afterglow of brilliantly successful productions of Gilbert and Sullivan's "Pirates" and "Gondoliers" shortly after Anne came into post, reflecting a slightly lighter touch to what was performed on stage under this new regime. Stage shows represented just one of Bill Walker's phenomenal range of extracurricular interests and he soon became involved as stage manager. He has fond memories of Jimmy Chisholm (later - *inter alia* - Jimmy Blair in Take the High Road and Wishee Washee in the Eden Court panto) as the Duke of Plaza Toro in the Gondoliers. In the same show Rob Seymour and Peter Kelly, of the highly talented musical family who were regarded as Inverness's answer to the Von Trapps, as the two brothers.

Country Club activities also changed little, with trips to Cantray fish farm, the Royal Highland Show and Burnetts' Bakery included on the programme in a year when George MacKenzie was Chairman and Suzanne Ross secretary. Among Patsy Forbes' assistant leaders was Bill Walker.

There were ups and downs of course but Jane Graham, Jim Sim and Marjorie Melvin did their level best to keep Scripture Union membership going during those mid-70s. Similarly while the Orienteering Club's membership is described as having increased in 1975, just a couple of magazine editions later sees club leader Jim Brennan (inventor of the carrier bag!) referring to "not a good year", despite having within its ranks some of the school's better runners such as Rosalind MacLennan, Rona MacKintosh, Andrea Mitchell and Mirren Ramsay.

Into the 1970s, the magazine's traditional summaries of the year's activities died out. There had been a long tradition of the school very much keeping in touch with its former pupils and staff with successes, retirals and deaths in particular recorded on an annual basis.

Although so many features of the school flourished up at Culduthel, one tradition which regrettably died out was that of the School Magazine which disappeared in the early 90s. It was a tradition which had begun in the late 19th century with The Academical and from the 1920s had continued with distinction in the form of the school magazine. The only exception had been the war years where shortage of paper and resources forced temporary halts.

But the 1972 edition gives an interesting resume of what went on during the session which ended that June. This was Ian Fraser's first as Rector and also the first ever during which Inverness Royal Academy, with no S1, did not have a six year secondary department.

The now traditional visit to the Edinburgh Festival, with 72 pupils involved, was the highlight of the early part of the session. Then on their return, Ian Fraser was installed as Rector on September 6th. Later that month the Schools to University conference, another hardy annual, took place before Allan Wilson took a group of Maths pupils to Aberdeen for a course on the then novel discipline of computing.

In October a party escaped the Highland autumn on a Mediterranean cruise on the SS Uganda while November saw Graham Lilley win a bronze medal at the Scottish Schools swimming championships.

ORIENTEERING

Back row: Kenneth Docherty, Jock Ramsay, Colin Chisholm, Neil McLachlan, John Murchison, Sandy Tasker.

Middle row: Mr Brennan, Mirren Ramsay, Margaret MacLennan, Jill Mathers, Stephen Clark, Fiona McMillan, Sheena Gordon, Alison MacLennan.

Front row: Catriona MacCallum, Jean Arthur, Linda Garden, George Gunn, Dorothy Garrick, Linda Wilson, Elena Duff.

The annual school fete took place, as usual, just before Christmas at which point the History department also showed Eisenstein's film "Battleship Potemkin" about the Russian Revolution.

The entry for March refers to *"the local catastrophic though spectacular burning of the Playhouse, and the national calamity caused by power cuts"* (a consequence of the miners' strike against the Heath government). However, it also comments that these disasters did not prevent a successful month at the school.

Four pupils – Graham Quinney, James Grant, Rory MacPherson and Bryan MacGregor of the 3rd Inverness Company – won the UK final of the Boys' Brigade Stedfast Magazine national quiz in London. In so doing they upstaged the author who, two years previously in a team which included fellow Royal Academy pupils and 1st Company members Alan Watt and Tombo Reid, had missed out on the same honour by a single point in Cardiff.

The school's other swimming star Martin Shore, by now in Sixth Year, also gained a schools international place.

By the early 70s, much of the pomposity of earlier decades had disappeared from school magazines. But the entry for June still comments that *"to prevent the post examination inclination towards indolence, pupils will be involved in an exhibition by three Senior Secondary Schools to pronounce our exultation at 100 years of compulsory education."* The resume of that month also heralds the annual visit to the Pitlochry Festival Theatre as well as prizegiving attendance becoming optional for the first time.

This may well have been a decision enforced by the demise of the Playhouse which made the new venue the school hall. With parents and guests present as well as pupils, this would have been some way short of being able to accommodate a full house. This change also meant that my own final 1971 prize giving day crocodile of pupils going down the Brae and along Eastgate and Hamilton Street towards the Playhouse (in earlier years the Empire) had been the last ever.

Staff departures that summer included Ian Bowman from Music and Alan Dougherty who was leaving the English department to go to the Examination Board in Edinburgh. The 1972 magazine also includes a deserved tribute running for a page and a half to Jess Thomson whose valedictory on retiring from the Classics department had so impressed Bill Walker and many others. Jess's association with the school went back to 1913 when, with Archduke Franz Ferdinand still alive and well, she began as a pupil in the Primary department. Then in 1930, the year the Great Depression started, she returned to begin a teaching career which would last for 42 years and make Room 4 a shrine to all things Latin and Greek.

When I made my appeal for FPs' reminiscences they included the following from a boy who left in 1974, but whose request for anonymity I am pleased to respect.

"I was in Curly Stuart's French class along with Davie Milroy and I remember Curly once saying to Davie that he was speaking French with a Clachnaharry accent. I don't think Curly was meaning to be complimentary. (Davie has, since I received these memories, cheerfully admitted this to me! – author.) *I was also in Hairy Hugh's Chemistry class when the syllabus changed. Hairy Hugh didn't agree with this and decided to continue teaching the old lessons. That was why he explained to us interesting facts like how to make fireworks instead of the proper lessons – I never did get my Higher Chemistry.*

"I very much appreciated Chunky Hamilton. I had no natural abilities in any sport but Chunky always encouraged me as I gave 100% at whatever sport was on offer. I remember him saying once to me after cross country 'you are never going to be a star but you certainly have stamina'. He was exactly the same with others. He encouraged the triers and I felt he disliked those who didn't put in the effort.

"In my view the best teacher that I had was Mr Wilson of the Maths department. He coaxed the best out of everyone. He also had an interesting way of dealing with homework. After setting everyone their homework, next day he would ask if anyone had not done it. Anyone admitting to this would get a punishment exercise. But every few days he would follow up his question by going round to check if anyone wasn't telling the truth. If he found that someone had not owned up, there would be a much greater punishment. There were some in the class who learned a good deal about probability from this method."

One very significant features of my weeks as a student teacher there in 1975-76 was the link up I was able to make with a group of highly talented athletes. They had raised the school's game considerably from the mediocrity which had prevailed, and of which I was part, during my own pupil days. These emerging stars were now senior pupils who were not much younger than I was and against whom I used to compete from time to time, so common ground was easy to find.

Top of the pile was Donald MacMillan who was the first athlete I ever coached and who, after moving on to become a veterinary student in Edinburgh in advance of setting up practice near York, became a full Scottish internationalist at 800m and 1500m. Don has held Inverness Harriers' club records in these events for 30 years now. As a 15 year old, he beat me for the first time in a 400 at the Nairn Games in 1976 – albeit with a start in a handicap race but at a time when I was North of Scotland champion. That was possibly the episode which first made me start thinking that coaching might really be more my thing.

Then came hurdler George Coghill, sprinters Duncan Chisholm, Dougie Phimister and Simon Fraser and distance runners Wilma Brownlee (who at the time of writing is still racing her daughter in half marathons) and Mirren Ramsay. They and the next generation of Royal Academy athletes, the first at Culduthel, would go on to play a key role at the start of Inverness Harriers' transition from an insignificant provincial club to a major force in Scottish athletics. Much of my involvement in that began during that teaching practice month of February 1976 when we would head off on training runs round the Crown once classes were over at 4 o'clock.

During that four week placement, I also had the experience of being in the crowd of over 3000 at the Northern Meeting Park which watched

Nairn MacEwan's Highland Rugby Club defeat Selkirk 20-0 to win promotion to Division 1 of the National Leagues. The game, featured on Rugby Special with Bill MacLaren commentating, grabbed the imagination of the whole of Inverness and as a sporting occasion certainly ranks with much of what Caley Thistle hosted in the years to come.

It was with considerable regret that I ended that four week sojourn at Midmills to return to the tedium of educational theory at Aberdeen. Then that May there was a major breakthrough at that annual cattlemarket where local officials go round the colleges allocating posts to students. It was here in Aberdeen that Divisional Educational Officer Ivor Sutherland offered me a job teaching Maths at Millburn which was in the process of transition from junior to senior secondary school as Inverness's protracted comprehensive rearrangement continued.

I accepted it gratefully. Ideally I would have preferred Chemistry at Inverness Royal Academy, but I knew there was nothing available. On the other hand there was at least a definite hint from the DEO that such a post might well emerge at the new Culduthel building which would be welcoming pupils in S1-3 from south Inverness and its landward area a year or so later in August 1977.

There was also another interesting and encouraging element to that interview. They say that left handed people are particularly good at reading upside down and on the sheet of paper in front of Ivor Sutherland I could clearly see that I had had a recommendation from John MacLeod, my old Dalneigh headmaster who was now Assistant Director of Education.

At the end of June 1976, Inverness Royal Academy held its annual prize giving in the school hall at Midmills. This was a rare occasion when three Rectors appeared on the stage together and would not be repeated until the prize giving of 2011 when Alastair McKinlay was the incumbent, his predecessor, the recently retired John Considine was the guest of honour and also in the platform party was Robin Fyfe who had been Acting Rector during the interregnum.

In 1976 it was Ian Fraser giving the annual report, W. S. Macdonald, now a Highland Regional Councillor for North Caithness, the honoured guest and D. J. in the Chair. So 17 years on from the staid 1959 affair in the Playhouse described in Chapter 2, there had been two changes of Rector while D.J. was now performing the role of Col MacKenzie and W. S. was the new Miss Young!

It is at this point that I will reveal that I am an expert on Ian Fraser's end of session addresses! The reason is that, of the 22 he gave, I was the official timekeeper for 15 – and for 15 of John Considine's 16 as well. To explain briefly, at my first Royal Academy prize giving for seven years in

1978, I benefited from beginner's luck and won at my first attempt the staff sweep to guess how long the Rector's prize giving speech would be. This led to my being handed the job of organising the sweep the following year - which I then did, with four different incumbents, for the rest of my career with just a single gap in 2004.

At that 1976 prize giving Bruce MacPherson, acknowledged as brilliant not only by Bill Walker, was presented with the Dux medal and the Howden Medallists were Roddy Innes and Rose Rollo.

According to the Courier's account, the Rectorial address began with a report that the roll in this four year (S3-6) school had been 798, an increase of 16. However a further hike to 860 was expected next session when the intake from Millburn would be 260 – the largest to date, which would stretch both accommodation and course choice availability.

That in itself is revealing since less than a decade previously the selective intake from the whole of Inverness and a large part of the County had been less than 200. Now it was 260 only from east Inverness and its immediate hinterland, chosen on the basis of Higher prospects determined at Millburn. So it was clear that, although a form of interim selection still existed, this was at a considerably lower level than before. Ian Fraser also reported an 82% pass at "O" Grade and 77% at Higher, both significantly above the national average. This was unsurprising given the school's long academic tradition and still a degree of selection but it's one of his latter remarks, made little more than a year before the new building at Culduthel opened, which raises eyebrows. Speaking of Inverness's transition to comprehensive education, the Rector of the town's oldest school which was undergoing radical change felt obliged to preface his remarks with "The situation as I understand it is this….".

Such a remark does not inspire much confidence in the certainty with which the Education Committee was proceeding nor in how it was briefing its senior figures. However, what the Rector did follow on with was indeed an accurate estimate of how things would ultimately unfold.

It is also ironic to read the Rector's confident statement that a phase two would be provided for the new building due to open at Culduthel in 14 months' time. It would not take long for that pledge from the Education Committee to become the colony of "temporary" second hand huts which will be well into their fourth decade of service there by the time they are demolished, at last to be replaced by the new school building in 2016. A more detailed account of how the Culduthel building evolved, or failed to, after construction began is given in Chapter 5.

A rather squint programme page from The Gondoliers – Christmas 1974 – run off on our rather aged Gestetner duplicator. Technology would improve.

<u>DRAMATIS PERSONAE</u>

DUKE OF PLAZA-TOFO .. .. James Chisholm

LUIZ (his attendant) .. .. Gordon Tocher

DON ALHAMBRA DEL BOLERO . .. . Neil MacArthur

MARCO PALMIERI) .. .. Peter Kelly

GUISEPPI PALMIERI) .. .. Robert Seymour

ANTONIO) .. .. Charles Forbes

FRANCESCO) Venetian . .. .. Robert MacGregor

GIORGIO) Gondoliers . .. .. William Fraser

ANNIBALE) .. .. James McAllan

DUCHESS OF PLAZA-TOFO .. .. Marianne Mackintosh

CASILDA (her daughter) .. .. Laura Turner

GIANETTA) .. .. Ailsa Swan

TESSA) .. .. Carol Sinclair

FIAMETTA) Contadine .. .. Dawn Taylor

VITTORIA) .. .. Norma Elliot

GIULIA) .. .. Monica Spence

INEZ (the King's foster-mother) .. .. Carol Robertson

ACT I

The Piazzetta, Venice

ACT II
(3 months later)

Pavilion in the Palace of Barataria

That roasting hot summer of 1976 also saw a debate in the letters column in the Courier about what the school should be called in the new comprehensive era. The two contributors had three features in common - they were Royal Academy FPs, they abhorred the comprehensive principle and they remained anonymous.

On July 13th the first correspondent loosed off a salvo against comprehensive education. He or she also seemed to take a dim view of the prospect that what had just become Millburn Secondary School would, by the dropping of the "Junior" label, in practice become "Millburn Academy" just like its neighbour. This was what eventually also became reality.

But then a week later, the second anonymous contributor really rocked the boat by proposing the following viewpoint: *"As a former pupil of Inverness Royal Academy and proud of its traditions of selection and academic learning, I view with horror the proposal to combine this name with the new school at Culduthel. This will be a fully comprehensive school and the only qualification a pupil will need for entrance is that of living in the catchment area. All former pupils of the Academy must unite and insist that the new school is called Culduthel High School and let Inverness Royal Academy die an honourable death."*

The Editor's note from Eveline Barron, whose uncle Evan Barron was a leading light in the old Boys' Club and a significant school historian then reads: *"Surely it is many years since anyone could choose or be selected to attend Inverness Royal Academy. It seems to have been a 'district comprehensive' for some time."*

The writer of the letter itself, who seems to have been sufficiently upset by the proposed changes to want the term "Academy" completely expunged from the educational vocabulary of Inverness, clearly failed to understand what could become possible in terms of achievement and tradition in a local comprehensive school. In this connection, the next two chapters will reflect what has been achieved at "Culduthel High School". Indeed it will even be argued that in many ways the comprehensive version significantly outshone earlier selective and fee paying formats in the field of sport.

This second correspondent also very conveniently chose a very short period on which to base their case. The "tradition of selection", which was held up as so virtuous, in effect only really operated fully during the 25 year long Promotion exam era up to 1970. It had existed partly before that through County Scholarships and similar bursaries and for six years afterwards in the revised entry criterion of studying for one or more Highers.

Totally ignored was that for the large majority of its history, the main method of entry to Inverness Royal Academy was the means to pay fees which carries no more virtue than any accident of residence. It also seemed to be conveniently forgotten that the cerebrally challenged progeny of affluence had for long also loomed large on the roll in an earlier era.

However, his viewpoint does resonate with the reality that Invernessians took quite a few years to understand that the new building was in fact Inverness Royal Academy. It was not unusual at all in its earlier days to hear it referred to as "Culduthel Academy" if not "Culduthel High". This also squares with a letter I received many years ago from an expat FP who said that one of the reasons he was delighted to have received a copy of the original "Up Stephen's Brae" was that he thought Inverness Royal Academy had gone out of existence in the late 70s!

Then in a sense, Eveline Barron's response is even more elitist since she appears to have been suggesting that this institution, now only serving east Inverness and with a widened intake, was already some years down the road to damnation!

When it was finally confirmed that Inverness Royal Academy would become a comprehensive, there was also a viewpoint that it should acquire Millburn's building and a catchment area round about. Meanwhile Millburn would be located at Culduthel and serve that catchment. Certainly this would have given the Royal Academy a larger proportion of private housing in its area and this may have been one of the motivating factors, but the idea never got off the ground.

My summer of 1976 ended at Millburn where I began a very happy session teaching Maths and finding out what comprehensive education and mixed ability teaching were all about. I had already had a taste of Millburn that June because, on discovering that I would be going there in August, I arranged to spend my final teaching practice there. The Head Teacher Willie Weatherspoon and my Principal Teacher Ruaridh MacDonald were especially supportive in these very first days.

It was here also that Colin Baillie, who had become one of Millburn's first Assistant Rectors in the 1973 changes, gave me my first independent commission in collective athletics coaching. He put me in charge of the First Year "B" team at the Inter School Sports – but from little acorns! It was also here that I found that the only way to communicate with Baillie was to trail behind him, breathlessly saying your piece as he rushed inexorably about the place, seemingly doing half a dozen things at once.

My teaching commitment in my debut session included three First Year classes which were all Culduthel-bound the following year. I have sometimes wondered if the Millburn timetablers knew even then that I was probably moving on and sought to provide a bit of continuity. As it happened elements of all three of these Maths sections appeared in my

Science classes at Culduthel the following session, which added further continuity. My Millburn timetable also included two mixed ability Second Year classes and, in these glorious days when it enjoyed the separate status it still deserves, "O" Grade Arithmetic classes in both S3 and S4. The year of familiarization with mixed ability teaching, including less able pupils, was extremely valuable.

Even though I had shared Dalneigh Primary with contemporaries of all abilities, streamed into 7A, B and C, six years in the Stephen's Brae Ivory Tower followed by four more in an even higher one in Edinburgh had left me less than familiar with the intellectual challenges of many lower ability pupils. It was a steep learning curve, but one which would give me a head start on the Royal Academy's existing staff who would have to contend with a sharp culture change at Culduthel from August 1977.

I also found out how to use a Banda duplicating machine with its A4 template from which you physically scraped away the wax surface with a sharp point to make your image before turning the handle. To users of laser printers and Powerpoint presentations, such technology will be unrecognisable. However this wasn't my first experience of Banda reprographics because Allan Wilson used a machine to make freshly duplicated notes for our Higher Maths class. On receipt of them, many of us would then spontaneously "snort" each page which smelled strongly of the alcohol solvent.

In these days there was also an urban myth that this device had been invented by Dr. Hastings Banda, the then President of Malawi. This was at a time when Dr. Banda was regarded as an extremely decent chap in the UK, especially up North where he was even an Elder of the Church of Scotland. It was only some years later that I woke up to the reality of a repressive dictator who was given a good press in Britain because of his Western leanings in the Cold War.

Once permanently back in Inverness I was also instantly able to resume the much more regular involvement with Inverness Harriers of my pre-student days. I bought my first car as well - a pretty basic Simca 1300 from Inverness Motor Company for £875. The man who sold me it was Ian MacKenzie, one of Archie Fraser's and Tom McCook's fellow First Years back in 1958 and eventually proprietor of the 147 Snooker Club.

At least I was luckier than Archie whose identical model would, a few years later, spontaneously combust as he played in a staff football match at Walker Park. Suddenly someone appeared and asked "Does anyone own a green Simca". When Archie replied that he did, the response was "Well it's on fire!" By the time we rushed over, it was well alight and all we could do was to call the Fire Brigade. It emerged that the cause of the conflagration was an electrical fault but the car – mercifully I would suggest – was a write off.

What is Jimmy Johnstone (Abdul) saying about (clockwise) Torquil MacLeod, Alan Findlay and Jim Sim?

Weekend visits to that ultimate 70s Inverness social hub The Hayloft in Eastgate also became more regular than in student days. Even on a probationer's take home monthly income, which was all of £168, they also became that much more affordable.

The upper bar in the Hayloft was an amazing, seething place on a Saturday night in the early to mid-70s. It was thick with cigarette smoke, a pint cost about 25p and I don't think I have ever experienced a pub where it took so long to get served. However, the clientele seemed extremely patient, even before licensing hours were extended to 11pm in 1976. 10pm closing meant that revellers were in danger of being back out on the street by quarter past, either having binged from about 9 or with hardly a drink drunk. With places like Dillingers Night Club still a couple of years away there were few other places to go unless someone had got a carryout.

To return to Millburn, its year groups in S1 and S2 were massive with over 500 pupils in each. In S1 there were no fewer than 19 teaching classes, of which I had three – 1F, 1N and 1X. There were two buildings – the original 1961 structure and a somewhat newer and larger neighbour - supplemented by a huge colony of huts which even Culduthel would never match. Some of them eventually ended up at Culduthel after Millburn's roll began to drop. At the period change it was all but impossible to battle your way through a seething mass of humanity in the bottom corridor of the new block where my Room 6 was. This was because Millburn was, in effect, holding junior pupils for three of what would become Inverness's five senior secondary schools.

Apart from those who would leave in 1977 to become the Royal Academy's new S2 and S3 at Culduthel, there were also pupils at Millburn from the Culloden and Ardersier areas since the new Culloden

Academy would not come on stream until 1979. That was an interesting scenario in itself, and warrants a brief digression for the ultimate Royal Academy trivia question - "Who is the only former pupil to occupy the Rector's office at Midmills?"

It's a slightly trick question since no Royal Academy FP has ever become the school's Rector. The answer is actually Derek McGinn, who had been a pupil in the 50s. Derek was appointed Assistant Rector at his old school in the mid-70s and in 1979 became the first Rector of Culloden Academy. With Derek in the office by the front door, Culloden Academy occupied Midmills for a year until its own building in its own catchment area was complete. However when we spoke about this, Derek did reveal to me that *"as a pupil of the D.J. era, I felt very strange sitting in that chair!"*

But even the first tranche of departures from Millburn to the new Royal Academy building at Culduthel meant a substantial drop in roll there and hence a reduction in staffing. This led to almost 20 transfers to Culduthel, which of course was what Ivor Sutherland had anticipated when he dropped that heavy hint at my college interview.

Some of these transfers - including my own - were voluntary and indeed applied for. But others were compulsory which did upset one or two of the less willing. I think there was still a perception among some of the younger Millburn staff in particular that the Royal Academy was just that bit stuffy, traditional and not quite ready for the brave new world of comprehensive education.

Inverness Royal Academy's move into that brave new world is the subject of the next two chapters, but during the two session overlap between Culduthel and Midmills, I was able to sing my swan song in the old place during 1978-79.

For old time's sake, I was really grateful to Jim Dunlop for giving me the opportunity to have my very first Higher class and a share of the Sixth Year Studies with himself for that final session down in Midmills.

This was also a gesture with long reaching consequences. Because when Doug Morrison retired in 2011, I became the only survivor in the profession who had taught classes in that Midmills building where I was a pupil and about which I have written all these books – apart from the one period a week Ross Finlay used to fill in for Eddie Hutcheon. So in that sense I am the last of a generation which lasted for 84 years.

There was quite a strange atmosphere about the place during that final session, now three years on from my return as a student teacher. For a start, the place was half empty since all that were left were Fifth Year, who would complete their schooldays at Culduthel, and the very final Sixth Year to go through the place.

This meant that all that remained was a pretty mature clientele – another step on from the mid-70s when S3-6 had been in residence. So the atmosphere was like what I would imagine a Sixth Form College to be, with even less youthful variation than before. Among staff and pupils alike, there was the steadily increasing feeling that the end of an era was very much upon us.

So with Millburn just along the road also shrinking after its mid-70s boom, Frankie Jew's profits from selling sweets and single cigarettes must similarly have been in decline as pupils migrated to Culduthel and Culloden. It is also a sobering thought that Midmills' youngest inhabitants will, at the time of writing, all be into their 50s.

One of a number of poignant valedictories to that building was the very final senior dance in the old assembly hall in December 1978 - a function appropriately named "The Last Waltz". In the years immediately following the publication of "Up Stephen's Brae" in 1995, a few year groups invited me along to their reunions to deliver a light hearted after dinner quiz on the old school. These included that final Sixth Year – I believe in 1999 to mark the 20th anniversary of their departure.

Katie Rennie was the very last Head Girl of Inverness Royal Academy in the Midmills Building in that 1978-79 session, with Malcolm Booth as Head Boy. In the years after she left school she spent time in both Galashiels and London, but always came back to her home town where she is now settled with a family as Katie Gibb. Her career has included time in retail management and as a Dan Air hostess when that airline used to fly out of Dalcross and she now works for Children 1st (the working name of RSPCC). She has especially strong memories of the old school being a sparsely populated place in its latter days.

"Towards the end there were far fewer pupils there than there had been before. It was just ourselves, the Sixth Year, and the Fifth Year who moved up to the new building to finish off their education. You felt you had the school to yourself which was quite sad and actually quite eerie. These were the last days of the old ways when teachers wore cloaks and we held doors open for them. I hope they felt we had respect for them. Younger pupils make a school come alive, but we didn't have any of them left by the end. All we were focused on was exams when we got to Fifth and Sixth Year and we missed their carefree adolescent energy.

"When it rained, buckets started appearing all over because the roof leaked in various places, especially above the walk way on top of the library.

"As for the teachers, Miss Rose was just a star and so was Mr Johnstone with his matching bow tie and handkerchief. He had a quest to achieve a style and he never failed in that. I had a bad car accident in 1976 and spent a lot of time in hospital and I will never forget Miss

Shepherd the German teacher who came and taught me in her own time to make sure I didn't miss too much. She had a passion for teaching which was unbelievable and so did Miss Banks my Maths teacher. She could just give a class a look and they would be quiet. She never needed to raise her voice. We once had a new boy in from London who thought he could take advantage but he was very quickly put in his place by Miss Banks. I still regularly see Miss Allan who recently advised me on growing sweet peas – the advice and teaching never ends!"

Since 1979, prize givings have taken place in the theatre at Culduthel. It was the morning after the very first one – and hence our final act of session 78-79 – that Morton Roer and I drove down to Midmills in my Humber Sceptre which had just become a replacement for the now thankfully discarded Simca.

Our mission, at her request and invitation, was to clear Margaret Murray's Lab 17, to share the proceeds between us and either bin the rest or put it in storage. In the spring of 2010 I decided to tidy out the Culduthel chemistry store room. Here I came across items of ancient, possibly 19th century, glassware still wrapped in the Press and Journal from June 1979.

So 30 years on, I was again reminded of that expedition and of my final departure from the place on official business on its last day as part of Inverness Royal Academy – once more through that boys' door into the Midmills Road car park.

And now, with the Midmills era over, it is time to look at what Inverness Royal Academy then evolved into.

5 - CULDUTHEL – A NEW BUILDING AND A NEW EDUCATION

In the autumn of 2012, momentous news broke as I was drafting what was originally conceived as a short chapter about life at Culduthel within this final volume of Midmills reflections. On 26th September the Scottish Government announced that Inverness Royal Academy was one of a number of school rebuilding projects it was going to support and that it would be part funding a brand new school.

This was final confirmation that, after years of campaigning, we really would be getting a new building. Construction would, like similar projects at Dingwall and Millburn, go ahead in the grounds of the existing premises. It was scheduled to begin late in 2013 or early in 2014. As a result, at some point in 2016 Inverness Royal Academy should now move into its fourth building since the school opened in 1792, although of course Midmills acquired three added phases between the 1920s and the 1970s.

With this latest episode of school history about to close, there immediately emerged a need for Culduthel to get rather more attention in this book than originally planned, so the next two full chapters are therefore on that subject. This is by no means a definitive history of Culduthel but, in the spirit of the earlier books, more a series of personal reflections of 36 years there.

The Culduthel building did not take long to deteriorate after it opened in 1977. In particular at a relatively early stage – indeed within about five years – Inverness Royal Academy discovered that moving out of Midmills did not mean an escape from leaking roofs. It also didn't take long to invite the conclusion that the construction was not, for instance, of the same quality as Charleston and Culloden Academies which, by the early 80s, were both also up and running in Inverness. I always saw something painfully ironic in the name of the firm that built Culduthel - The Lesser Construction Company.

By the late 2000s the state of the fabric had become parlous in the extreme and calls – some of them very public – were mounting for something to be done. In particular Dave Henderson, an FP of the Midmills era who at the time was a local councillor, became so outraged at the condition of the place that he branded it "a slum" at a Council meeting. Inevitably this became instant front page headlines in the local press and the label stuck until something was eventually done.

I believe that this single outburst on Dave's part was a significant factor leading to the eventual decision by Highland Council to do something about the problem. Not only did it focus public attention on a rapidly deteriorating fabric, it also created a slogan for the local media who had now as a result become well and truly focused on the question of accommodation for Inverness Royal Academy.

The moment Dave used the word "slum", I became convinced that this was an invaluable hook to which the media could and would attach themselves. That was confirmed by a conversation I had with the Press and Journal reporter who had attended the meeting where Dave made the remark. When the word popped out, she and her Courier counterpart simply exchanged very knowing looks. The next day's headlines had already effectively been written.

Eventually some Academy staff became well and truly fed up with the regular and very public use of the term "slum school". But my view was that this was a necessary evil, well worth the temporary pain for the long term gain. And so it transpired.

Lengthy investigations began into the state of the place and the big issue then became whether Highland Council would merely recommend an upgrade - or the new school everyone wanted. After what seemed an eternity of over a year, it was eventually announced at the beginning of September 2012 that the Council would seek top-up funding from the Scottish Government for a complete rebuild. Then at the end of that month, Holyrood revealed that it would provide around half the cost of what would be a £34 million project with the Council supplying the rest. In March 2013 provisional plans were publicly revealed along with a commitment that construction would start mid 2014 with completion two years later.

The original Culduthel building, which is now to be replaced, opened on schedule for the start of the new session on Wednesday August 24th 1977 – but only just. Tradesmen were still hard at work right up to and past the deadline. Just days before it was due to welcome its first pupils, the place looked, literally, like a building site with wood and wires and plumbing lying all over the place. Indeed in the current era of obsession with health and safety it is likely that hundreds of pupils and staff would never have been allowed near the place for some time to come.

But these were the 70s so everybody just piled in and got on with it. And since the place was completely new to everyone, we all got well and truly lost for days since very few people knew where they were going.

Despite the physical chaos on site, the move to Culduthel had been the subject of months of logistical planning among the staff and there was far more system in place than might have appeared, with "Jack the Janny" and Derek McGinn in the thick of it.

Archie Fraser, as Principal Teacher of Biology, was very much involved in that flitting from Midmills to Culduthel which began in the summer of 1977 and really lasted for the entire two years of the split site. His recollections are of a pretty orderly affair which was well planned.

"The flitting went pretty smoothly I thought. In the end we just emptied the place and certainly all the Science stuff went with us whether we needed it or not. The new Culloden Academy moved in after us for a couple of years and their teachers were heard to complain that we had left them nothing at all! As it happens, Derek McGinn, who was about to become the first rector of Culloden but was still an Assistant Rector with us at that time, was pretty instrumental in our flitting and did a very good job.

"Some teachers at the new building had more experience in teaching mixed ability First and Second Years than others but the three heads of Science had all done that kind of thing before. Bill Walker then Jim Dunlop then myself had all taken up our posts within a couple of years in the early 70s and we had all done that kind of thing before so we managed to put together the new Science courses quite well."

An orderly transfer is also the recollection of Leo Longmore. *"I really didn't find it too disorganized at all although it was hard work over the summer and I rather enjoyed teaching in both schools,"* she remembered.

Everybody instantly pulled together and got on with it, but there was one seemingly lost soul. Bill Murray was on the point of retiring and the appearance was that this was a man who in many ways had epitomized the traditions and values of the old place and really wanted nothing to do either with comprehensive education or with this new building. However some contractual anomaly meant that Bill was unable to retire until the end of the month, so had to spend that final week commuting between the two buildings oiling the wheels. It was very evident in conversation with him that he really wanted none of it.

The departure of Bill Murray after 26 years at the school in a sense drew a line under the old regime just as the new one was on the point of birth. In many ways Bill epitomized the values of "the old Academy" and his views to a large extent resonated with some of those expressed in the Courier's letters columns the previous summer.

It was also an apparent anomaly that the greatest disquiet about the school's departure from a more rigorously academic ethos should come from a man, hugely respected, who was synonymous with a department which, at the time, still had no academic component at all.

The catchment area's four major town-based primary schools – Hilton, Lochardil, Holm and Cauldeen – provided most of the building's intake into the first S1 the school had had since 1970-71. But the new Inverness Royal Academy catchment area also served the landward area which brought in country pupils from the likes of Aldourie, Stratherrick, Farr, Foyers and some rural primaries which have since been closed for lack of numbers. Inevitably this meant that a fair number had quite lengthy bus journeys from locations such as Whitebridge and Gorthleck. So when

Opening Ceremony – Official Programme

Highland Regional Council Education Committee

****

Inverness Royal Academy

(CULDUTHEL BUILDING)

Formal Opening

by

Dr. D. J. Macdonald
Formerly Rector, Inverness Royal Academy

on

Thursday 20th April 1978, at 2.30 p.m

winter weather closed in, it was – and still is – quite common for these rural pupils to be sent home early or not to appear at all.

On the other hand in the 70s closure of the entire school due to a snowfall was extremely rare. This was despite the first two winters after Culduthel opened being extremely severe with exceptional amounts of snow. The first months of 1979, which elsewhere saw Inverness Thistle's Scottish Cup tie against Falkirk at Kingsmills Park postponed a record 29 times, were especially bad. However the school remained open in weather conditions which would certainly have seen teaching abandoned two or three decades later.

On one occasion early in 1979 during his Sixth Year, Don MacMillan came up to Culduthel to go for a run with me and we decided to beat an ambitious path up Leys Brae. Hardly half a mile up the road we found ourselves battling our way through a fresh fall, along a narrow channel of ploughed snow, claustrophobically built up well above head height on both sides of us. Nowadays I would be required to complete an extensive risk assessment if embarking on such an expedition with a pupil.

There were even occasions when Stratherrick hill and the narrow lane which then ran between Dores and Stratherrick Roads were both impassable. The latter has now been replaced by part of the Southern Distributor Road. In the snow of the late 70s that lane quite easily became a no go area for vehicles in general, and my less than dynamic Simca in particular.

This was an era when a "new ice age" was being predicted by some climate scaremongers. It would not take very long for views to change completely and for the term "global warming" and "climate change" to enter the vocabulary.

During one very snowy early Culduthel session, the school was due to reopen after Christmas on an inhospitably early January 4th. The only way I could get there from where I lived in Dores Avenue was to pack some clothes in a bag, sling it over my shoulder, and run the two miles or so up the hill.

The Rector, however, always relied on his car. Or at least he did so until the very rapid thaw which saw Culduthel Avenue extensively flooded - with his Triumph 2000 well and truly stranded at the deepest point in front of a vast audience in the rooms on the north side of the building.

Culduthel is a strange building with the lift right at the far end along with the science staff base and the library. This was because the original intention, as the roll rose, was to build a "Phase 2". This for a short time was even a common, albeit increasingly optimistic, term in the school's vocabulary. It was planned to be built in a westerly direction towards Holm Mains so strategic services like the lift would then become far more central.

View over the huts from Room 55 in 2013. There was a lot less to see in 1977!

However, Phase 2 never materialized. One significant factor would appear to have been a change to Inverness County Council's original plan in the early-70s to have a school of 2000 pupils, built in two stages. It was on this basis that construction began and was forecast to continue into Phase 2. Then in the mid-70s Scottish local government was reorganised and the new Highland Council was more inclined to limit the size of its establishments. So, at a time when both Culloden and Charleston Academies were also on the way, Inverness Royal Academy's Phase 2, which had been intended to include a swimming pool, was cancelled.

Instead, as the roll steadily rose towards 1300 in the early 80s, additional accommodation was provided in "temporary" huts. These were not new and arrived from Millburn, now downsizing, and Portree. They will only disappear over 30 years later with the rest of the building when the new one opens. However those who have taught in the huts over the years have often expressed an amazing affection for them. It also took very many years even to get the area around them covered in tarmac.

Consequently the sea of mud which used to develop around narrow slabbed walkways out there every winter would have enabled the History department to re-enact the Battle of Passchendaele.

Science, including Physics before the huts were built, was based on the top floor and we seemed to have a plethora of chemists. In addition to the original establishment of Jim Dunlop as P.T., Sheila Martin and Margaret Murray, Dr Helen Wood had briefly joined the department and then I was transferred from Millburn.

But so was Dick Langridge, even though he was really a Biologist and did eventually revert to that. Douglas Tosh was also recruited fresh to the school, as well as Bill Francis who left after a year and was replaced in Room 53 by Morton Roer. Morton was our new A.P.T. Science and then succeeded Jim when he retired as Head of Department in 1994. In these early days, and especially during the discontent of the industrial action of the mid 80s, the dividing door between 53 and 55 was a regular and welcome two way conduit for "getting it off your chest".

Bob Boardman replaced Bill as PT Physics on Bill's promotion and remained for almost 30 years. That was in huge contrast with the 16 years up to 1979 when there had been no fewer than four Physics PTs. Dr Charles Edward Stuart, who later returned to Inverness as Highland Council's Director of Education, was succeeded by Andrew Halkett and Jim Wilson. Then there was Bill (famously referred to by Maude as "the head of my department") who, at seven years, was the longest serving of these four PTs Physics.

Meanwhile Archie Fraser, like Helen Wood a PhD, was by then about three years into three decades as PT Biology. One of Archie's star pupils in his early days at Midmills had been Sue Black who went on to become one of the country's most famous scientists as Professor of Anatomy and Forensic Anthropology at Dundee University. This led her to make a number of high profile investigations and television appearances and she frequently and publicly gave Archie a lot of credit for her getting where she did. On one occasion she also came to Culduthel to give a memorable lecture on her work.

I was allocated Room 55, a rectangular area of some eight metres by five, located between Room 53 and a large toilet. Inspired by The Fonz in "Happy Days", I came to call this toilet "my office" since it was from there that, once mobiles came on the scene, I would latterly deal with a lot of my phone calls to and from the media as school press officer. Room 55 is also opposite Room 52, from which Jim no doubt felt he could keep benevolent tabs on someone who was still just entering the second half of what was then two year probation.

At the age of 24, one seldom thinks too far into the future. So I doubt if it ever occurred to me that I would be the sole occupant of Room 55 as my professional home for the next 36 years. This means that, having lived in several different houses during my lifetime, I have without doubt spent far more waking hours within the confines of Room 55 than within any other set of four walls.

I daresay that Room 55 back in that era of "Grease", "Saturday Night Fever" and the embarrassment of the Argentina 78 World Cup looked brand sparkling new, just like the rest of the school. As I write this passage whilst actually seated in Room 55 and look around me, I find that quite difficult to believe of a room which got one fresh coat of paint roughly half way through its 36 year lifetime.

Its most striking original feature was the absolute forest of utility points which sprouted out of every conceivable surface. There was a plethora of sinks each fed by three water taps, and of pairs of gas taps and appendages which carried eight electricity sockets each.

This was a case of vast overkill because there were far, far more of these points than any class of 20 pupils could conceivably need at any one time. Over the years many of them were progressively removed or became defunct. The quality of the plastic plumbing was so dreadfully poor that by around 2010 just two of the original multitude of sinks still worked and some had to be replaced to make practical work possible.

There was also the frequent problem of blocked plastic sink traps and leakage into Room 35 below me. This was partly because it is as impossible to prevent kids from putting rubbish down sink holes as it is to prevent the constant disappearance from a lab of two items in particular – spatulas and crocodile clips. Then there was the ongoing dispute about who was meant to clean out the sink traps, with janitors and technicians both denying all responsibility. This meant that overflowing sinks and stinking traps became a regular problem.

The gas supply at Culduthel remains an anomaly. When the school was built it was right on the outside of town and not very near any existing gas main. This meant that the gas supply had to be, and has remained, propane from tanks at the back of the school. So while most schools use North Sea gas which is methane, we still have supplies of propane delivered by tanker. Litre for litre, propane needs two and a half times as much air as methane to burn, so special Bunsen burners with appropriate air holes were needed.

Propane is also about one and a half times as dense as air, so soon sinks. This sometimes meant small quantities catching fire at bench level if a tap was left on. And it created mayhem in Bob Boardman's hut 68 on one famous occasion. Bill Walker well remembers not only the sensational fate which overtook Hut 68 but its sequel which also put paid to its semi detached neighbour.

Room 55 – latterly with rather fewer utility points.

"A notable incident in hut 68 was caused by the heating system automatically switching off at 6pm which created a spark in one of the heaters. There had either been a gas leak or someone had left a gas tap on and a lot of gas had escaped. The gas, being propane, was more dense than air so sank to the floor where it was caught in the spark and ignited. The cleaner had just locked the door when there was this huge explosion. She turned round seeing the windows flying past her: she was very lucky not to be caught in that. The explosion also started a fire and for weeks the equipment in Room 68 reeked of smoke.

"A few years later there was the second fire which started at about 4am and was spotted by a passing taxi driver who called the fire brigade. I was called in at about 6am. It was the summer term after the exams. The room's fire extinguishers and computers were seen having been hastily covered in grass on the bank across the playing field so it was clear that the fire had been started deliberately by a criminal act and on this occasion both huts 68 and 69 were badly damaged. About 18 months later someone was arrested on the basis of fingerprints found on the equipment."

Huts 68 and 69.

Although just one teacher occupied Room 55 for all these years, a vast number of pupils have passed through it, giving scope for an interesting back of an envelope calculation to produce a rough approximation.

It's reasonable to estimate that each year I had on average seven classes. And let's say that each class, as against a maximum of 20 for a practical section, had 18 pupils. That's around 126 pupils a year, but let's also say that each pupil's stay averaged two years. That is probably the least precise of these figures but while some would only stay for a year, others would be with me much longer such as Kirsty Roger, who eventually went on to become a GB under 23 heptathlete, who was in my class from S1 through to CSYS.

Two years seems a reasonable ballpark average stay so instead of multiplying the 126 by my 36 years, we only multiply it by 18. That actually comes to 2268, but given the fundamental imprecision of this calculation, I think it's reasonable to suggest that "over 2000" pupils have passed through that single classroom during my occupation of it. A further extension of this back of an envelope calculation then produces the result that Room 55, since 1977, has been occupied for more than half a million pupil hours. That is worth mentioning even as a tribute to how incredibly hard wearing the original orange floor covering has been! On the other hand how many pupil hours have some of the rooms at the front of the Midmills building accommodated since 1895?

What a variety of humanity has passed through Room 55 in terms of shape, size, ability, personality and all the other variables which the human race encompasses. When you have been a teacher in a comprehensive school for almost four decades you really have seen a great deal of life - the very good, the very bad, the joy inspiring, the downright tragic, the highly normal and the downright eccentric are just six extremes which could begin to circumscribe the experience.

It's probably even more difficult to enumerate colleagues, of whom hundreds will have taught at Culduthel during its lifetime. From the old building, Allan Wilson would remain as PT Maths until 1987 and Eddie Hutcheon continued as Head of English for five years after that. They would be replaced respectively by Norman Morrison and Phil Ellis. Donald MacArthur, who was also a former hostel warden, was another who had transferred from Millburn. Whilst still teaching Maths, Donald was promoted from PT Guidance to a long line of Assistant Rectors. These also included Ken MacIver, Ken Allan, Jean Godden, Mary Gillies, Duncan MacQuarrie and the current set of redesignated Deputes - Gordon Piper, Alex Gunn, Robin Fyfe and Pauline Brady. Over time the school has undergone minor structural changes such as to what started life as two "quiet rooms" off the main staffroom. There were further changes to the original, communal Assistant Rectors' room which was converted into a series of separate cubicles and each depute now has private accommodation.

The departures of two successive rectors could not have been more different in nature. Ian Fraser's retiral in 1993 had been foreseen for some time and his 21 years in the job culminated in a going away party in the Craigmonie Hotel which was memorable for one or two reasons.

Then in total contrast, it was at the end of term staffroom Christmas party in 2009 that John Considine dropped a bombshell and announced that he would be leaving us almost immediately after the holidays to take over as Highland Council's Head of Education. Robin Fyfe then stood in as Acting Rector until that August when Alastair McKinlay, whom I first knew as a young and enthusiastic PE teacher with Tain athletics teams in the early 1980s, arrived from there.

Ross Finlay, Pauline Brady and I latterly became the final trio of survivors of those who had taught at Culduthel from day one in 1977. This followed the departure of Doug Morrison and the formidable Rena Fraser, who began as a Maths teacher, then became PT computing and achieved early retirement only to return as chief invigilator in succession to Connie Sutcliffe.

I had already spent a year teaching mixed ability classes at Millburn which turned out to be valuable experience. It meant that when Culduthel opened I was in that respect actually a step ahead of a number of existing Royal Academy staff, some of whom had been my own teachers less than a decade previously. There were quite a few with no experience at all of teaching anything other than academic pupils and for some, mixed ability came as a severe challenge. Indeed I will hold my own hands up and admit that, despite my flying start, it took me quite a few years fully to appreciate the difficulties that many non-academic pupils can have.

The principle of mixed ability teaching is that, in theory, all the classes in a year group should have more or less the same distribution of abilities across the range from top to bottom. Inevitably this means compromises, especially at the extremes, even if differentiated material is used. My experience has also been that this is a system which begins to break down once individual differences become more marked into S2.

The other problem I encountered with mixed ability teaching is that with the best will in the world it seems very difficult to get a representative distribution in each and every class. Some classes, although nominally mixed ability, perform much better than others and that's before the addition of any additional constraints such as grouping pupils together for the purpose of Learning Support or the teaching of Gaelic.

Learning Support, or Support for Learning as it is now called, was something completely unfamiliar to many of the old Midmills staff. Beginning as "Remedial" with Margaret MacLeod and Sheena Beaton running the show from a couple of rooms at the bottom end of the science corridor, it developed hugely over the years. Then, as requirements expanded, so did staffing with a flood of additional teachers, including Liz Taylor as its first PT. There was also increasing and very valuable backup provided from staff currently designated Pupil Support Auxiliaries.

The department also expanded physically and took over Room 51 which had previously been a Science lab. One of its early occupants had been John Christie who then left science teaching for the ministry and ultimately became Moderator of the General Assembly of the Church of Scotland.

I used to feel especially sorry for poor Maude who had taught bright kids academic Physics in the Ivory Tower at the top of the brae since just before Hitler invaded Poland. Now, almost 40 years later, when it became impractical for her to have a full timetable at Midmills, she had to spend part of her time up the road in this concrete culture change. And it wasn't just the educational upheaval.

4M1- 1990.

In the old days, Maude regularly used to advise colleagues of her three aims in life - a fur coat, a car and a man. The garment was duly acquired and furthermore Miss Maude Yule was into her 40s when she became Mrs Ian Anderson. Then when the car, which was driven everywhere at 18mph, came on the scene it was parked right at the back door of Midmills leaving Maude with, literally, 30 yards to walk to her seat in assembly and then a further 20 to Lab 21.

In cruel contrast, the car parks at Culduthel, especially the front, are a day's march away from the building so it really became a major effort for this "big wumman", now in her 60s and with a history of knee problems, to make her way to her new classroom on the very top floor where Physics then was. As a result there really were days during the mercifully short period she suffered this before her retiral when I felt sorely tempted to say to her "you look exhausted dearie!"

My first year at the Royal Academy, session 1977-78, was spent entirely at Culduthel teaching S1, 2 and 3 and my classes included a number of pupils I had had for Maths at Millburn the previous session. Now, as a

Science teacher, I found myself once again having to come to grips with "flying solo" in a subject for the first time. It was probably here that my baptism of fire from Jim Dunlop during that pre-college placement two years previously really came into its own.

In Third Year it was "O" Grades for those deemed capable or a non-certificate course designed by individual departments for the rest. We had Topical Science (inevitably dubbed "Tropical Science" by the pupils) and General Science. Here you could mess about with whatever took your fancy because there was no Scottish Certificate of Education Examination Board to be accountable to and a lot of good work was done.

First and Second Year Science came from a publication called "Curriculum Paper 7" which laid down what had to be taught in fourteen sections. The last time the sciences had been taught in S1 and 2 at Inverness Royal Academy was at the beginning of the decade when it was separate Physics, Chemistry and Biology. Now it was what was known as Integrated Science although much of the course was pretty easily identifiable as one or other of the three separate disciplines. Shortly after the millennium, another of these educational full circles was completed and the three separate sciences were reverted to once again before the Curriculum for Excellence decreed another U-turn.

Mention of "Section 6", which was very much Biology, tended to inspire nudges and winks in this less enlightened era since this was the sex education section. This is now taught by all science teachers to all pupils and also featured extensively over the years in the Personal and Social Education curriculum. It all represents massive progress since an the earlier age of Miss Annabelle Duncan of the Alliance of Honour giving highly secret talks on "growing up" to Second Year girls only.

Then there was Section 2 about living things. Here I had the idea of asking my pupils to take in their own pets so we could investigate their various features. This would have fitted into the present day Curriculum for Excellence very well – except that the health and safety industry would probably take a pretty restrictive view of kids bringing pets into school. Back in the late 70s I used to have a regular array of cats, mice, gerbils, budgies, rabbits and even a ferret in various containers which kids had taken in with them.

On one occasion a pet rabbit managed to escape and I was very late for my athletics coaching session in the games hall by the time it had been coaxed out from behind my equipment cupboards. Someone else brought a pet pigeon which also escaped into the class and eventually lodged itself on an upper ledge. The poor thing must have been quite scared too, since the stream of incontinence which it liberated ran down my wall and stained it for nearly 20 years before the decorators' next visit.

Just as spectacular, but not brought in by any pupil, was the bat which many years later got into Room 55, possibly through my fume cupboard chimney. Eventually it was apprehended by Ruth Black the technician using a butterfly net.

The pigeon didn't cause the only blemish in my new room. With my very first "O" Grade Chemistry class I decided to demonstrate the manufacture of soap on one of the back benches. This involves boiling an immiscible blend of fat and concentrated sodium hydroxide solution and the first time I tried it, I overheated it just a bit. The upshot (literally!) was that the mixture boiled suddenly and fired a great gob of this pernicious stuff skywards. Inevitably it hit the ceiling and as I prepare finally to vacate Room 55 in 2013, I imagine that I can still see the outline of where it struck the tile back in 1979.

Middle Corridor.

Not long after that, I had my first Higher class at Culduthel making esters. For the benefit of non-chemists, these are sweet smelling organic substances made by mixing an alcohol with an organic acid, adding a small amount of sulphuric acid as a catalyst and leaving the mixture in a hot water bath for about 20 minutes.

The original Culduthel chemical store, which has now been an art staff base for years, was at the far end of the science corridor – another symptom of the proposed Phase 2. With great effort I lugged trays of acids and alcohols along to my room one Friday morning and, without inspecting them too closely, told the class to help themselves and get on with making some esters.

What I didn't know was that one of the trays contained a bottle of butanoic acid which, despite being a reactant for making pleasant esters, itself has a most disgusting smell reminiscent of rancid butter and vomit. Unfortunately I was completely ignorant of its presence until the entire room had been filled with this ghastly odour. It was instantly on everybody's clothes, so stopping that particular group's experiment was no more than a token gesture.

To rid the classroom of the putrid pong, I came in over the weekend and placed dishes of concentrated ammonia about the room in a fortunately successful attempt to get rid of the stink through neutralization by the alkaline vapour. But nothing could be done about the horrible whiff permeating all our persons.

It was also the period before lunch, which created an obvious problem in itself. Then there was the additional issue of one boy called Alastair – or more specifically his dog Hughie who was well known about the streets of Lochardil. Alastair was just heading home for lunch where, as usual, he expected to be greeted by Hughie. What concerned me was my additional understanding that the smell of butanoic acid was one of the things that made girl dogs attractive to boy dogs, so to speak. And Hughie most definitely fell into the latter category.

To the infinite amusement of the rest of the class, I did warn Alastair of the potential snag when he got home of possibly being mistaken for a girl dog. So when he came back on the Monday to a Room 55 which by now was only reeking very mildly, I rather anxiously asked him what had happened?

It was to my great relief that Alastair reported to a class in stitches of laughter that when he went into the house, Hughie actually ran away. We could only conclude that Alastair was stinking so strongly of butanoic acid that the poor pooch had thought he was being assailed by a whole battalion of girl dogs and had taken flight in panic.

For the two sessions 1977-79 that the school operated in both buildings, it was inevitable that staff would have to make many journeys between teaching commitments on both sites. Some used their own cars and were paid travelling expenses while there was also a shuttle minibus driven by a janitor. The other measure that had to be taken was to offset the timetables between the two premises to avoid having to allocate whole free periods for travel.

At that time a 9am to 4pm school day of nine 35 minute periods was in operation so the 15 minute assembly or registration took place at Culduthel at the start of the day at 9. Then at Midmills it was switched to the end at 3:45, with classes starting straight off at 9. Assembly at the end of the day felt really strange even to me so must have been really unsettling for those who had taught there for years.

What the timetable offsetting did was to allow 20 minutes travelling time for anyone going from Culduthel to Midmills, but a slightly tight 15 for those going in the opposite direction. Patsy Forbes was one of a large number of these commuters between the two buildings and remembers the rush to get from one to another.

"I do recollect that at least one member of staff was caught speeding because it could be quite tight," she said. *"There was one year when I had double Fifth Year at Midmills on a Friday and then had to get up to Culduthel to teach First Year. There was one day when there was a lot of snow and I was just coming out of the school gate when I had a puncture. Some people helped me change the wheel but by then it was just too late."*

Archie Fraser was another teacher with somewhat fraught memories of commuting between the two buildings.

"On one of my journeys between the two buildings I was outside the Green Drive Post Office before the roundabout was put there and a bucket from a vehicle owned by Fraser the contractor hit my bonnet. It was that same green Simca as went up in flames when we were playing football at Walker Park so it must have been jinxed. The driver gave me his firm's phone number and they told me to go to a garage near Tomnahurich Street and it was duly fixed there but I don't think I had a lot of luck with that car."

Physics Club 1983

Bill Walker remembers both the rush up the road and minibus service at a time when his domestic arrangements were also in a state of flux.

"When we moved from Midmills to Culduthel a lot of things were in boxes to be taken up the road, but not only in school - at home as well because I moved house just a week previously so that was quite a busy time. For the couple of years when the school was split between the two buildings, I only had the Sixth Year Studies to teach at Midmills and I used to commute between the two buildings. Sometimes I would take my car but other times I would go in the grey minibus which Pat Haughey the janitor drove between the two sites. The seats were parallel with the direction of travel so every time you went round a corner passengers and anything else they contained would always slide along them."

This commute also became my own lot in that very last Midmills session of 1978-79 which included that notorious Winter of Discontent in advance of the May 1979 General Election which saw Margaret Thatcher installed in Number 10 as Britain's first woman Prime Minister. During that same winter, there were times when we never knew whether the school was going to have electricity or become the latest victim of power cuts.

The three years from August 1979 saw the very final stages in the eleven year evolution of Inverness Royal Academy from the town's selective school to a local comprehensive. That month it once again became a single site establishment, but now at Culduthel. The first dux of Inverness Royal Academy to have received an entirely comprehensive education was Elizabeth Murchison in June 1980 and in the years to come, many pupils went on to realize major academic achievement.

Then in August 1980, after the departure of the last pupils who had come up the road from Midmills to complete their Sixth Year, every pupil was now a product of the comprehensive system. By August 1982, once all of those who had started at Millburn had gone, for the first time since I had left in 1971, Inverness Royal Academy was a six year secondary with an entire intake which had arrived in First Year and had passed right through. However, minor qualification should perhaps be made there to account for the pupils, many of them hostel dwellers, who came to Midmills in S3 from junior secondaries in outlying areas such as Harris, but also as close as Beauly.

During Margaret Thatcher's three terms as Prime Minister between 1979 and 1990, her Conservative government came up with a number of changes to education in Scotland. One of these was school boards, the brainchild of Scottish Secretary Michael Forsyth. This, we initially believed, was conceived as a means of using parent power to beat teachers over the head in retribution for the industrial action of the mid-1980s and to diminish the powers of local authorities.

But school boards never really turned out that way and the only one in the Highlands which used its power to depart local authority control was Dornoch Academy, largely because it didn't get its own way from Highland Regional Council. In practice school boards generally had very good relations with professionals in the establishments they served so any intended political purpose never materialized. This continued until they were replaced by parent councils which continue to fulfil a successful and supportive role – at Inverness Royal Academy at least.

Then there were league tables of exam results and other parameters, which still exist at least in some form. These were sources of considerable misinformation and had the capacity to be very divisive. Unfortunately, if I have to criticize journalists, I would have to observe that in general their understanding of educational matters is often not very good. In particular they tend to take a far too simplistic Daily Mail-like view of what league tables tell them. In particular they are too ready to dismiss schools with difficult catchment areas as "failing".

In general, league tables tend to tell you at least as much about the school's catchment area as they do about the school itself since catchment area-related factors are arguably even more influential than those relating to the school. As a result, many schools have been over estimated and many more have been unduly criticized on the strength of misunderstood exam results. However, across the entire period I have taught at Inverness Royal Academy I believe that the school has done a good job in terms of the results it has achieved. This applied both before and after the Munn and Dunning reports led to curriculum change and the replacement of "O" Grade by Standard Grade in the 80s.

What I taught in the classroom over the years in some ways never changed, but in others evolved with the times. The nature of Chemistry as a subject means that you can't get very far without early attention to the likes of the structure of the atom, ions and valency and that is as true in 2013 as it was in the 70s or before. Similarly, in S1/2 it is difficult to wait too long before an introduction to energy, but here the treatment of it changed over the years along with society's attitude to it.

I have always been a great believer in placing what I am teaching in context. As a result I always taught radioactivity to Higher pupils in the context of the short 20th century from Henry Moseley's death in the 1914-18 war to the lifting of the threat of nuclear war on the collapse of Communism around 1990. A favourite story after 1985 was the French secret service calmly entering Auckland harbour and sinking the Greenpeace ship Rainbow Warrior because it had been interfering with their nuclear bomb tests in the Pacific.

Similarly I would not explain structure of the atom to Third Year pupils in isolation, but would also trace the origins of atomic theory back to the ancient Greeks. Here, with the benefit of the History of Science course I did in Second Year at Edinburgh, I was keen to highlight how the Greeks came up with the idea of the atomic elements of earth, air, fire, water and the ether in the fifth century BC.

Then there were almost two and a half millennia of nothing being discovered at all about the structure of atoms before the sudden and glorious dawn of the most exciting period of all when it must have been simply wonderful to be a physicist. Just 35 years elapsed between Thomson discovering the electron (1897) and Chadwick revealing the neutron (1932). During that short period, thanks to the likes of Rutherford, Bohr, Heisenberg and Schroedinger, so much light was shed so quickly on the nature of the atom and quantum mechanics was born along with Einstein's theories. This is a theme which I also developed further when we began quantum mechanics in Sixth Year Studies.

On the mention of J.J. Thomson, I would never fail to name drop and tell classes that I had met his great grandson Ben, who was an international decathlete, in the Drumossie Hotel at the wedding of Neil Fraser, of whom more in the next chapter.

As for energy, my teaching career began in an era of concern about what would happen when the oil ran out. It ends amid efforts to replace fossil fuels because of their environmental implications. Standard Grade came along in the 80s, just as Margaret Thatcher had declared herself "green" in response to an upsurge in the Green Party vote. Being green was suddenly trendy, so the Standard Grade Chemistry course had lots and lots of stuff in it about acid rain.

I have always encouraged pupils to think critically rather, for instance, than accept unthinkingly various assertions about climate change and human activity which have become modern day orthodoxy. So if electric and hydrogen powered cars are "good", then surely it is worthwhile to ask where the electricity to power the cars and make the hydrogen comes from? The challenge was to find a convincing answer which does not lead back to fossil fuels. I would also challenge them to justify biofuels in terms of any extra photosynthesis and hence carbon dioxide removal capacity conferred upon the planet, as opposed simply to providing an alternative crop on agricultural land which merely contributes to increased food prices.

I would float for discussion the proposition that the root cause of human-induced climate change is not carbon dioxide but in fact humans themselves. They produce the produce carbon dioxide, and indeed also create demand for other essentials such as food and water. So is the fundamental difficulty not therefore population?

Bearing that in mind, my next invitation was to consider the role of that self-appointed environmental paragon, ex-US Vice President Al Gore. As the father of no fewer than four fossil fuel-guzzling American children, Mr. Gore's personal worsening of the problem on which he has lectured loud, long and self righteously to others therefore needs to be examined very critically indeed

Another aspect of the classroom which evolved hugely over the years was humour. In this respect, I latterly began to find myself more restrained in the one liners I could get away with as Political Correctness tightened its malevolent grip.

Humour has also become dated as I discovered, possibly in the 90s, when I trotted out my well tried line *"I mentioned it once, but I think I got away with it"* - and nobody laughed. This of course is Basil's classic follow up to the immortal words *"Don't mention the war!"* in "The Germans" episode of Fawlty Towers. It suddenly dawned on me that here now was a generation to whom Fawlty Towers meant at best very little. Most really hadn't a clue what I was going on about which did make me feel just a little bit dated. But I really had no interest in replacing my repertoire with material from Big Brother or other reality shows. Along similar lines, whilst teaching about compounds called "diols", references to telephones now meet with blank stares.

By the 90s, the age had well and truly passed of Corporal Jones bellowing *"Don't panic!"* in Dad's Army and the Pythons' conviction *that "No one expects a Spanish Inquisition"*. Memories were fading of Mr. Humphries' camp confirmations that he was free, or of Frank Spencer having another *"Oops Betty"* moment. And Strictly Come Dancing was still three decades away when Brucie first declared *"Good game, good game"* before seeking the *"scores on the doors"*. Options for amusing and topical one liners hence receded. But not even in a much less PC era would I ever have risked Sergeant Major Shutup's description of the Concert Party in "It Ain't Half Hot Mum"!

This was also an era of physical punishment which was abolished in the mid-80s. I could embark here on a lengthy moral discourse on this. Suffice it to say that my attitude towards "the belt" has changed considerably over the years, especially more recently. In the early years I found myself an infrequent user of it when it was part of the established order. Its disappearance didn't really inconvenience me very much. However, on balance I initially disapproved of that edict on the grounds that no effective substitute sanction was available. On the other hand I stopped using it myself quite by accident. A couple of years before abolition, I loaned mine to a colleague, it was never returned and I found myself managing perfectly well in its absence.

Even now, there is still no substitute sanction but I look back on these days with a good deal more distaste and regret, apart from the most extreme cases. That may seem like a dramatic conversion but it is hardly as Damascene as that of the female AHT from a certain Scottish school I once heard of. For years her job description had included "Belter In Chief - Girls". Then shortly after abolition she was heard deploring the "beating of children" in a talk to a Woman's Guild!

However, on meeting, many years on, those to whom I did apply it, I have never detected any hostility to my having inflicted on them a practice which earlier generations took as part and parcel of the system and an occupational hazard of education. On the other hand more recently I have been met with near disbelief on some occasions when the belt has come up in conversation with younger people.

Recently acquired distaste aside I still have a wry smile about the time I returned to my lab from the Technicians Room to discover that one of my first S3 "O" Grade class in session 1977-78 had gone missing. It emerged that the boy had hidden in an equipment cupboard at the back of the room in my absence, and as such had actually put himself at some risk. A couple of strokes of the implement acquired from Mr Dick of Lochgelly were administered amid massive amusement throughout the class and I still believe that the recipient's hero status significantly numbed his pain.

Just days before this book went to print, I bumped into the same boy, now a photographer and a 50 year old parent, at a parents' evening in the school. We shared several reminiscences and, bearing absolutely no grudges, he proudly left Room 55 with a photo on his phone of that cupboard still in its original place.

6 - CULDUTHEL BEYOND THE CLASSROOM

The Royal Academy at Midmills had always been served superbly by a rich programme of extra curricular activities. Bodies as diverse as a Film Club, Outdoor Club, Country Club, Scripture Union and a lot more supplemented a whole range of options in sport and music. Many of these activities made very rapid and successful transitions from Midmills to Culduthel so the new building was very well placed to hit the ground running in that respect. One tradition in particular which continued in the best of form was the stage show. Anne MacIntyre was justifiably confident that anything that could be done among academically selected senior pupils could, with a suitable change of repertoire, also be achieved right across the age range in the comprehensive set up.

One of her earliest efforts at Culduthel was a lavish and outstandingly successful production of "Joseph and the Amazing Technicolour Dreamcoat" which was performed just before Christmas 1979. By now the whole school, including the ex-Midmills Sixth Year, was on the one site which helped greatly. On this occasion, although up to the ears and beyond in coaching athletics, I thought I would like to have some limited involvement with this production. However, any notion of limitation evaporated at a very early stage.

As a work, this stage musical is scarcely in the same league as "Dido and Aeneas" or "Cosi fan Tutti", both performed down the road at the beginning of that decade. But "Joseph" was still musically quite complex with, in particular, sequences of bizarrely changing time signatures. It therefore came as something of a shock to be asked to rehearse the band. Although fairly well grounded in the theory of music, I find it difficult to read it at any meaningful speed so this would be a major challenge.

Maybe it was the confidence of youth, but I took the job on and was even listed in the programme as an "Assistant Musical Director". My solution to the music reading problem was simply to get an LP of a performance and learn the stuff from start to finish by listening to the disc over and over again whilst following a score. In fact to spare my parents the trial of hearing it *ad nauseam*, I used to take the LP, the score and my big, heavy Philips record player into my classroom of an evening to go through it all there. More than once I found myself singing along loudly to "Go, Go Joseph" or "Any Dream Will Do" - only to become aware that my cleaner was listening outside the door!

I was just one of a large number of staff involved in that production. Others included more or less the entire music department along with regulars from other departments such as Dave Ewan producing scenery, Isobel Allan in charge of costumes and Bill Walker nominally stage manager but fulfilling a whole lot more into the bargain. Apart from rehearsing the band, I also became something of an assistant stage manager and from there was drawn into the empire which was the Inverness Royal Academy Music department.

The weather intervened in the most ironic of ways. Trains weren't running past Perth because of the snow. So in order to get the camel costume which was being hired from Edinburgh and was absolutely essential, Isobel had to make a 200 mile plus round trip through the white hell on the then still "old" A9 so we could have that most iconic of desert creatures in our show. The camel was a huge hit though!

I did have a bit of a moral dilemma since I have always been quite resistant to pupils missing too many classes. That is a resistance which has possibly intensified more recently as departments and even individual members of staff have been held more and more closely to account for their STACS exam statistics.

But as my involvement with Joseph steadily increased, I found some of these reservations diminishing and even began to take whole classes, including occasionally my Higher class, down to the theatre so I could help out with rehearsals. That is something which in more recent years would have become unthinkable.

It was absolutely great fun doing the show where the cast included the twelve brothers, some of them ex-Midmills Sixth Year, the dancing girls and massive choruses largely recruited from among the juniors. Pharaoh was Steve Gibb, one of a laudable number of former pupils who went on to make names for themselves in the music business. Joseph, with an elaborate "coat of many colours" tailored by Margaret Currie of the Art Department, was Fourth Year pupil John Luke. As the production run in the Culduthel lecture theatre approached and rehearsals went from strength to strength, things were going brilliantly.

Until Joseph got a stinking dose of the cold!

We were absolutely at our wits' end since there can be few shows which depend more than "Joseph" on a single, central character. Then in the nick of time, Joseph made a recovery possibly more reminiscent of the New Testament than the Old and got himself "out of jail" so to speak. At the eleventh hour his voice just returned enough to allow him to croak his way through the run of performances.

It was something of a cross between Telly Savalas doing "If" and Lee Marvin's "Wandrin' Star". But it got us through what was probably one of the most successful school stage shows ever, playing to packed audiences. In fact "Joseph" was so popular that the run had to be extended to a fourth night and the public allowed into the dress rehearsal, with people still having to be turned away. Among the star turns were Murdo MacLeod and Archie Forbes as the "camel" and years later I came across a quarter inch tape recording by BBC Highland's Bill Sinclair.

Principals from the Joseph programme – apparently duplicated on the same intermittently disorientated Gestetener!

JOSEPH AND THE AMAZING TECHNICOLOR
DREAMCOAT

DECEMBER 1979

CAST

JOSEPH .... John Luke
JACOB .... Charles Sinclair
PHAROAH .... Steven Gibb
POTIPHAR .... Ian Kyle
MRS POTIPHAR .... Karen Hay
BUTLER .... Graeme Hay
BAKER .... Arnold Grier
REUBEN .... Kenny Ross
SIMEON...................... Victor Tough
LEVI....................... David Munro
NAPTHALI .... Simon Bignell
ISAACHAR .... Steven Dougan
ASHER .... Ross MacPherson
DAN .... Ian Beattie
ZEBULUM .... Jonathan Fraser
GAD .... Hugh MacLennan
BENJAMIN .... Kevin Barclay
JUDAH .... Frank Davis
CAMEL .... Archie Forbes
                       Murdo MacLeod

Within the next few years, Anne went on to produce the obscure but almost as successful "Parker Plan" which was invited to Eden Court for a second run. By this time I was stage manager in my own right and doing this at Inverness's main theatre was a memorable experience. There was even an attempt at "West Side Story" but that turned out to be a step too far and never reached the performance stage.

After he succeeded Anne as Principal Teacher of Music, Alyn Ross also went on to produce many more highly successful stage shows. These included "Bugsy Malone" in the 1990s, which created a huge impact across Inverness. We even managed to promote it through a press photocall involving the 1920s gangster characters with their splurge guns and a genuine period automobile.

One big asset the Culduthel building has is the purpose built theatre which greatly assists stage shows produced there. It is outside the theatre that the war memorials, translated from half way up the main stairs at Midmills, were mounted in the late 70s.

How the large wooden tablet for 1914-18 came into being is described on pages 32-33 of "Further Up Stephen's Brae". Buckie then inscribed handsome framed lists after World War II and the two have stood together ever since. It must have been after my parents visit to one early Culduthel stage shows – very probably "Joseph" - that my father first saw the memorial, and in particular the very last name in the World War II section.

That reads "Sgt John A Wilson – 51st HQ" which isn't entirely accurate, as my father then explained to me. He and John Wilson were fellow Sergeants at the HQ of 152 Brigade – one of three such formations which made up the 51st Highland Division. One day in August 1944 Brigade HQ was in a farmhouse near Lisieux in Normandy and it emerged that something was needed from the stores. After discussion with John Wilson, my father volunteered to run the errand. Seconds after he departed aeroplanes – tragically RAF in an incident of friendly fire – bombed the house. John Wilson was one of the fatalities. But for that 50-50 chance I may never have existed.

In 2011 I was asked to be the subject of one of a series interviews with local people in the Inverness Courier. In response to a question about my most memorable Invernessian, I quoted that anecdote and named John Wilson. Shortly after, the Courier received, for forwarding to me, a letter of thanks from John Wilson's daughter Barrie who had been a baby when her father died and herself became an Academy pupil in the 50s. Intriguingly she also enclosed a large and much better copy of the 1956 staff photo which I published on page 38 of "Up Stephen's Brae" after Patsy Forbes, who is in it, identified everyone else.

Ironically Barrie's mother and my mother, who by then had also become a widow, lived beside each other in the same block of retirement flats in Argyll Court in the 90s, but the incident was never discussed between them.

My experience with "Joseph" also led to a much increased and more general involvement with the Music department. For the next few years I was stage manager and general administrator for a variety of other successful productions both within and outwith the school. This created significant time demands in the face of my athletics coaching and there was also another musical departure which was a direct consequence of "Joseph".

Quite a few drinks had been drunk in Malcolm Wood's kitchen at the staff party after the final night when Anne proposed some inter-departmental cooperation between Science and Music within the classroom. She suggested that I might visit music classes to teach some of its scientific applications. Although not a specialist physicist, I said I would give it a go – and didn't even wake up the next morning regretting it!

The courses I devised gave Second Year music pupils an insight into the basics of sound in relation to musical instruments. Then further up the school the Higher Music class, where we also did after-school sessions, covered more advanced areas such as acoustics. That was supplemented by the mathematics of harmonics, diatonic scales and equal temperament, as illustrated in Bach's 48 Preludes and Fugues. This ran for much of the rest of that session and was so successful that we asked senior management for it to be officially timetabled. That, however, had to be turned down since the extra split site staffing allowance was disappearing at the end of that session. That had been carried on for one extra year after Midmills had been vacated and had given me some of the time I spent in the Music department. However its removal meant that staffing would be a lot tighter for session 1980-81.

As a post-script to the highly successful "science and music" educational experiment, I had to smile many years later when the Curriculum for Excellence came along. One of the things it seemed to trumpet as some apparent novelty was interdisciplinary learning between departments and subjects, which even received its own little CfE acronym of "IDL". The fact that there were teachers doing this kind of stuff 30 years previously was never really properly acknowledged in that brave new world of "novel" educational thinking of the early 21st century.

A still vivid memory of a major event on the world stage within days of the "Joseph" performance provides an illustration of how the global environment changed fundamentally during the Culduthel years. I went away for these 1979 Christmas holidays full of optimism for the future. I was looking forward to the athletics season of 1980 for which my charges were improving well, and also to a new association with the Music department which was developing directly from the "Joseph" experience.

Then in the dying days of that year and of the decade, the Soviet Union invaded Afghanistan and suddenly the Cold War took on an extra and much more sinister dimension. Within days some of that optimism was overshadowed by new fears of nuclear annihilation as rhetoric between NATO and the Soviets intensified. Although I have a vague recollection of the admittedly much more serious Cuba Missile Crisis of 1962, I am just too young to have appreciated its significance at the time. And while fighting in Vietnam may have been intense, hostilities never seemed to threaten to expand outwith South East Asia.

So this was the first conscious occasion in my lifetime that the Cold War had developed from being some vaguely unpleasant, unspecified background issue into what I perceived as a direct threat to my health, happiness and safety. This was no six week wonder either because we were now at the dawn of Pershing and Cruise missiles at Greenham Common in response to Soviet SS20s and this would cast a dark shadow over the next few years.

What we could not know at the time was that we were actually entering the Cold War's final phase. In another decade or so, the world would become a very different and much safer place following the collapse of Communism in Europe. Into the new millennium, the rise of Islamic terrorism would pose a new threat but the danger of mutual nuclear annihilation very much receded.

There have been corresponding radical changes on the home front during Culduthel's lifetime. The building opened in the declining years of Old Labour Socialist government. It witnessed almost two decades of Thatcherism and its aftermath in advance of the Blair era. Culduthel's replacement, one of the areas devolved from Westminster since the opening of the Scottish Parliament, was announced by a quite separately elected Scottish Government. Few would have foreseen that following the "No" vote in the 1979 Devolution Referendum.

Technological change over this period has been profound as well and one area which has been revolutionised is communication and the movement of information. In the 70s one of the most advanced items of school equipment was probably an electric typewriter in the "Secretarial Studies" department. Who would have envisaged computers in every classroom as part of an internet-led school network?

Things have come a long, long way since the 80s with BBC machines and other bulky looking gadgets and when a cassette had to be loaded on to a machine even to perform rudimentary tasks.

Inverness Royal Academy
Country Club

25th Anniversary

Programme
   Welcome
      Miss P.R. Forbes
   Toast to the Club
      Mr Hugh MacIntosh
   Reply
      Miss Christine Mackenzie

Drumossie Hotel   **September 11th 1981**

Reprographics, run by Morag MacBean from a glorified cupboard off the school office, initially amounted to a Gestetner type machine which couldn't be relied on to print straight and a single, creaky office photocopier. Individual departmental Banda machines further contributed to staff pigeonholes being permanently stuffed with paper in a manner now unheard of in this electronic age.

The large oblong blue card-covered register, which had to have its attendances balance both horizontally and vertically, is a thing of the distant past. Now attendances are recorded electronically and even the registration folder has become a museum piece. Exam marks are quite often kept on computer but I resist this as much as possible. I find that my marks book – with "Das Kapital" inscribed on its front cover (Marx book!) – does the job far more quickly and efficiently.

Computers are very helpful and welcome when they are of definite assistance. But we do tend to be far too uncritical of them, leading to far too many cases of using them for the sake of it. Emails by the thousand fly about the scholastic ether and maybe there is indeed a Parkinson's Law operating here. "Communication expands to fill the capacity to undertake it." Just about the only expression in the English language which challenges my will to live is an explanation beginning with the six words "You just have to click on....."

The school's immediate physical environment has also been transformed over the years. When it opened in 1977 the Culduthel building was right at the edge of town and all I could see looking southwards out of the window of Room 55 were the former Culduthel School and County Cottages. On the far side of the boundary fence was a farmer's field which I used to use to introduce the nitrogen cycle to "O" Grade pupils.

Then above the playing field there was the open country over which, into my 40s, I successfully pursued and got close enough to identify the former pupil who had been creating destructive mayhem in the school grounds during a show in the theatre. I did leave arrest to the police though! Beyond that, in the early days I could easily take non certificate classes out on a "country walk" direct from the school.

Now when I look out of that same window I see dozens, indeed hundreds of the houses which have been a major feature of Inverness's expansion. These have gradually materialized on the far side of the Southern Distributor Road which, around the turn of the millennium, forged its way through what used to be open country. The Brahan Seer, long before the advent of the Caledonian Canal, is said to have predicted ships passing behind Tomnahurich Hill. I certainly would never have foreseen heavy traffic making its way past the far side of Inverness Royal Academy. What used to be a rural location has now become well and truly suburbanized with additional features along that distributor road including two primary schools, a business park and two supermarkets.

Inverness Royal Academy had always been something of a sporting school with a number of successful performers among pupils and FPs. Sprinter Ian Young was highlighted in detail in "Further Up Stephen's Brae" for his double Empire Games bronze medal in 1934, two years before turning down Olympic selection in order to look after the family drapery business of Young and Chapman.

Then into the 60s and 70s, Martin Shore, for instance, was a successful swimmer while on the football field George Stapleton was a schools internationalist and Billy Urquhart became a full time professional with Rangers. However, I have always been a bit surprised at the sparsity of FPs of what regarded itself as Inverness's prime rugby school in the great Highland teams of the 70s which went straight from Division 4 to Division 1 of the embryonic national leagues. Alastair Hamilton, who was Bill's number two in the PE department and succeeded him as Principal Teacher, was a prominent member of that side. But there were relatively few FPs who went on from school teams to play for the town's adult club in its prime. The prevalence of students going away to university may have been a factor here though.

In complete contrast, Culduthel had not been open for long at all when there came on tap a sustained tidal wave of top sporting talent. Very quickly, and in a wide range of sports, Culduthel FPs were competing internationally, at Commonwealth Games from 1986 and in three cases even at Olympics between 1988 and 2012. The pair who began the whole process – which extends right through to the time of writing of this book in 2012-13 – both became pupils the day the Culduthel building opened its doors in August 1977. Neil Fraser had spent two years at Millburn before becoming one of the new S3 entry while Tommy Leighton came into S1 from Lochardil Primary.

I had run athletics sessions at Millburn and continued this on an even greater scale at the Royal Academy on Mondays, Wednesdays and Fridays after school. The talent which emerged was quite staggering, as was their receptiveness to hard work. Athletes like Maureen MacLeod and Chris Brogan quickly became Scottish age group champions with, among others, Eddie Leighton and David Allan, later the Scottish hammer champion, close behind them. But the two who first made it at senior level were Neil and Eddie's older brother Tommy who in 1981 became Inverness Harriers' first ever Scottish senior internationalists.

The seeds of that had been sown at Inverness Harriers and at our regular school sessions where the commitment of these athletes had done a lot to inspire me to want to coach the sport.

Gillian Ramage (Cattell) and the author with the 1983 athletics team. Hammer thrower David Allan (next to me) and high jumper Tommy Leighton (the tallest boy!) both became senior internationalists.

Tommy's selection in the high jump was quite incredible because he was still in the under 17 age group and competed for Scottish seniors in Gateshead just days after opening his "O" Grade results. By 1981 Neil had moved on from the high jump to the 110m hurdles and was still a Sixth Year pupil when he won the Scottish championship silver medal which gave him his selection six weeks later.

At the time there was still no proper track in Inverness. So coaching Neil towards the hurdles on the soft school blaes surface - which had been a disappointment from the start and will now become the site of the new school building - was a major challenge. For Neil, this was the first step in a process which would later see him compete in the 1986 Commonwealth Games in Edinburgh and the 1988 European indoor championships in Budapest as holder of the Scottish national record which would be his for seven years.

The athletes just mentioned, along with many others at the start of what was also a golden era for Inverness Harriers, made enormous contributions to school teams as well. The high water mark came in 1980 when Inverness Royal Academy pulled off a clean sweep of all eight team trophies across the South Highland Schools track and field and cross country championships.

In cycling, and of a similar era, were the Riddle brothers Roddy and Kenny, who were both in the road race in the 1994 Commonwealth Games in Victoria, Canada. Having reported on their cycling activities extensively both on the airwaves and in print, I have always felt extremely privileged that on the night they were told of their Commonwealth selections they came round to my house to tell me personally. I went on in later summers to interview them both as winners of the Highland Cross at the finish in Beauly.

Then there was Myles MacKintosh who had been Head Boy in 1994 and even by then was doing very special things in swimming. By 1998 he was an established Scottish internationalist and a member of the team which went to Kuala Lumpur to contest the 4 x 50m relay in that Commonwealth Games. And all of that even before getting to the three Royal Academy Olympians!

In the year group between Neil and Tommy was Eddie Alexander whom I first met in Maths class 1N at Millburn. A decade later Eddie had become a major track cyclist and a Commonwealth sprint bronze medallist at Edinburgh in 1986. Then come the Seoul Olympics in 1988 he had made further breakthroughs which took him into the British team and fourth place in the sprint at this supreme level. Fourth place, just outside the medals, is always the most painful outcome in championship sport. But Eddie's was a big achievement for British cycling, which would go on to produce Sir Chris Hoy in the same event a couple of decades later.

The next Olympian was Ewan MacDonald who arrived in First Year from Lochardil Primary in 1987. Ewan curled at Winter Olympics in 2002, 2006 and 2010 and would share Eddie Alexander's pain of missing out on an Olympic medal by taking that tantalizing fourth place. However, his main claim to fame has been his three curling world championship gold medals in 1999, 2006 and 2009. As a triple world champion, Ewan is arguably not only the most successful of a very distinguished bunch of sporting FPs but also the most eminent sports performer Inverness has ever had.

The third Culduthel Olympian, born in in 1985, was also the youngest by several years. Mhairi Spence took that golden era of Inverness Royal Academy sporting excellence, which began in 1981, into a fourth decade when she competed in the Modern Pentathlon at London 2012. Like Eddie, Mhairi was a former pupil of Holm Primary which can hence boast two Olympic representatives, and both under the same Head Teacher Roddy MacCrimmon.

It's strange how well I have got to know so many of the Royal Academy sporting stars at various stages. I coached Neil, whose best man I also became, and Tommy and followed all the rest at school. Then my paths crossed so often with many of them in later years as a sports journalist. Mhairi had also been a member of Inverness Harriers before moving on to that unique combination of swimming, fencing, horse riding, shooting and running. In addition she was, during her school days, a very good friend of both my daughter Jenny and my son Martin, so for various reasons I followed her progress with interest.

The first I heard of her was in 1997 from Roddy MacCrimmon at Holm School. He went out of his way to flag up to me that we had an excellent prospect coming our way later that summer. One school newsletter in 2001 records Mhairi's appearances in both the British Schools cross country international and the Scottish Schools swimming championships.

Her career was an interesting one since after some time at Modern Pentathlon's national centre of excellence in Bath, she experienced the frustration of being a travelling reserve at the Beijing Olympics of 2008. Then, just when selection for London 2012 seemed in the balance, she emerged spectacularly to win the world title in Rome that May and gain an automatic place.

What alarmed me then was that so many people instantly tried to hang the Olympic gold round her neck, which is the worst thing you can do. In the end a combination of some under performance and a rebellious horse in the equestrian event put her right out of contention even before a target malfunction in the shooting, so she eventually finished a gallant 21st.

For a single comprehensive school to have had three Olympians, two of them fourth placers, within quarter of a century is a truly remarkable achievement. But there were also so many more, a lot but not all of them mentioned here, who also did so well in the wider world of sport. It has been a golden sporting era which, who knows, may well continue.

Although athletics claimed the overwhelming majority of my time in extra curricular sport, I did manage to get an insight into other disciplines as well – especially after I became responsible for the school's media relations.

Minority sports like cycling, modern pentathlon and curling were by no means the only ones in which Culduthel FPs excelled. There was the famous night under floodlights at the Clach Park in 1994 when our under 14 football team won the North of Scotland Cup in a local derby victory over Millburn. That was a team which included Neil McCuish who went on to play for Clach among other Highland League sides and Scott Kellacher who had been on Celtic's books in his early teens and who became a coach at Caley Thistle. This was not the school's only North Cup win by any means but was one of the more memorable ones.

Neil and Scott sat for two years at the front of my Standard Grade Science class and had an uncanny knack of edging conversation with me away from what they were meant to be doing and towards football. One indicator of how close a community both the school and Inverness football can be is that almost since time began, Scott had been going out with Audrey MacDonald. Audrey was the younger sister of another well known player and pupil of a slightly earlier era, Danny MacDonald. In the due course of time Audrey inevitably became Mrs Kellacher.

The best known of many footballers I taught at Culduthel was Charlie Christie to whom, many years later, I would say: "Charlie, remember when you were a budding Highland League player in my Higher Chemistry class in the early 80s? Did either of us ever think that 25 years later I would be interviewing you on the BBC as manager of an Inverness team in the SPL?" Because that was exactly what Charlie did between 2006 and 2007, having previously and right from the start in 1994 been one of Caley Thistle's most influential players.

S1 athletics in bi-centenary year 1992 - many of them competed through to S6.

Returning briefly to the Midmills period, there have been strong links with shinty administration. Curly – Ellis Stuart – was a founding father of the Schools Camanachd Association. Then from the 60s John Willie Campbell, who taught Physics, and Ken Thomson and Archie Robertson, who were pupils, all went on to be Presidents of the main governing body The Camanachd Association.

One autumn Saturday afternoon in the early 80s, I decided to return to another of my roots. So off I set in a bus with Ron MacKay, then the junior member of the PE Department, and a couple of teams. Our destination was our old rugby rivals The Abbey School at Fort Augustus. Memories of trips to the Abbey have always been that bit warmer than those of visits to Gordonstoun. George Welsh, Gordonstoun's Head of PE, was a gentleman of unparalleled merit, but the institution as a whole never seemed quite as welcoming as the Abbey.

It was a generation too early for parallels to be drawn between the Abbey's Gothic splendor and the Harry Potter films. A trip there was always a very pleasant experience and the food, unlike Gordonstoun's, was excellent. This was my first visit to the Abbey as a teacher and it yielded a very interesting confirmation of rumours which had been rife among pupils for years.

Because yes – it was true that while the team went into the Hogwarts style dining hall for their fish and chips, the accompanying teachers were indeed diverted to another part of the school and supplied with drink by the monks who also staffed the place! It may not have been an irresponsible excess, but I have to say it was very welcome indeed.

Another major feature was the ski expeditions, both at home and abroad which Bill Walker also fondly remembers.

"There were Ski Club outings on Sundays to the Cairngorms and also foreign ski trips to Switzerland, Italy and France," he told me. *"The most unforgettable trip for me was in Easter 1985. That year, there was a particularly large group of 17 seniors who had been with the Ski Club from their first year. We had wanted to go to Les Arcs, the in-resort to go to at that time, for their last school trip. Just 3 weeks before we were to go, we were told we could not go there, but were offered Serre Chevalier which we reluctantly accepted. We were travelling there by bus. When we were on the ferry going across the Channel, we were told that we were not going to France, but to Italy, to Cesana Torinese. We got there many hours late at three in the morning.*

"As compensation, the following day, we were given Ski Passes for the 'Milky Way', allowing us to ski from Mongenevre to Sauze D'Oulx. It then became the most memorable ski trip not only for me and the staff, but also for many of these senior pupils. When I meet some of them now, it is often the first thing they talk about."

So Culduthel, both academically and in the sphere of extracurricular activities, actually did very well from a very early stage which quickly silenced the doubters. Many of these doubters were FPs, and their principal scepticism was that Inverness Royal Academy in its new status maybe just "wasn't up to the job". The vivid reality is that the "new school" – benefiting significantly from the traditions and values of the old – rose to the challenge with distinction, and continues to do so.

The front page of the June 1996 Newsletter, which completed my first session editing these publications, possibly best epitomises this. It carries a photo of 15 major achievers with their awards. Unfortunately, with the still limited technology of the era, the photo - headlined "A YEAR TO REMEMBER" - is of quite poor quality and not reproducible here. But it conveys an image of major achievement by a large number of pupils in a wide variety of areas both academic and non academic.

The article on the following three pages tells a tale of success ranging from Helen Mason winning the Highland Maths Jamboree to the pipe band becoming World Novice Junior champions and Sheena Murdoch, despite eventually becoming a doctor, winning a national engineering competition. Pamela Slinn, Kate Palmer and Elaine McGavin became Scottish schools champions in chemical analysis, a Royal Academy team captained by Marsaili Kerr won the Aberdeen University quincentenary quiz and there were sporting successes in disciplines as diverse as football, athletics, basketball and swimming.

These triumphs – academic, cultural and sporting - define for me what a school is all about outwith exam results. All of this also remained at a high level and featured prominently in an especially outstanding HMI report on the school published in 1997. On that occasion, the newsletter headline, and that of our press release to the media, was simply "A GLOWING REPORT".

I took over editing the Newsletter in 1995 when I became a Senior Teacher with responsibility for communications and media relations. In practice I had been the school's press officer since John Considine's arrival in 1993 for what would be 17 years in the Rector's office in succession to Ian Fraser who retired after 21. John was keen to see the profile of the school enhanced and I was glad to have both the journalistic background and media contacts as well as a strong commitment to help do just that.

It was Archie Fraser who persuaded me to do a minor U-turn on my decision of the 1980s not to seek promotion but instead to pursue a dual career in classroom teaching and journalism. Archie talked me into applying for that Senior Teacher post which gave me extra responsibility outwith the classroom and hugely enriched the entire professional experience of working at Inverness Royal Academy.

Few things quite capture the imagination of a school quite like being at the centre of attention on the visit of a major personality. Within a period of 11 years, no fewer than three visited the Royal Academy at Culduthel, one of them to return a further six years on. Prince Andrew's appearance was part of the bicentenary celebrations in 1992. Then Tony Blair took the place by storm in 2001 in advance of a somewhat lower key visit from Prince Edward who appeared for the first time in 2003.

The school's celebrations to mark the 200th anniversary of its foundation on July 16th 1792 created a lot of local interest, especially among former pupils of the Midmills era. At the time I actually thought that the response from some staff who had had no previous connection with the place was slightly muted and under the circumstances that was perhaps understandable.

A large programme of events included a dinner dance, an exhibition of school history, the production of an historical folio and a concert. But what especially caught the imagination here was when a request for a Royal visit from Prince Andrew, the Earl of Inverness, was granted and went ahead in June 1992.

One major part of the visit, which saw armed police swarming all over the place, was his coming to watch the school sports across the road on the field. My job that day, during my pre-press officer period, was starting the races so my day began by having my starter's pistol (a solid replica without even a hole for a bullet to come out of) checked by a member of the local constabulary.

As it happens, the cop in question was Alan Hards with whom I had worked in the Harriers for years, but procedures are procedures. I do have something of a regret that, purely for the sake of the visual effect, I didn't manage to arrange for a photo to be taken when, "gun" in hand, I was introduced to the Royal personage.

Across the road there had been a major pre-visit panic when, shortly beforehand, someone had come into the grounds overnight and sprayed the exterior wall with some extremely embarrassing graffiti. This was removed with the greatest of haste.

In the building itself Prince Andrew performed a ceremony which was the centerpiece and indeed one of the main purposes of his visit. This is an event which Bill Walker remembers especially well.

"Prince Andrew, the Rector, dignitaries, and myself were in the front concourse at the unveiling of the Bi-centenary Plaque. After the unveiling of the plaque, the Royal party were to move on to the theatre. I had, hidden in the sleeve of my academic gown, a walkie-talkie radio which, unfortunately, I had left fully switched on. In the midst of the unveiling, someone, I cannot recollect who, from the theatre, asked over the walkie-talkie where HE was, at which point, Prince Andrew replied "HE is on his

way". This was to much amusement all round and to the great embarrassment of one red faced Depute Rector."

"He" was also taken to the Library, through freshly painted corridors of course, to see the historical exhibition. This provided Ian Fraser with an interesting moment when he had to explain one of the exhibits to this former pupil of Gordonstoun School. The item in question was the hand bell which had been "liberated" from Gordonstoun in the mid-50s by one of our rugby teams in retaliation for post-match hospitality of that era, with which the players had been less than impressed. ("Further Up Stephen's Brae" pp 81-82.)

Hence the Royal visit wound towards a close and once Prince Andrew had gone, all the staff and various local dignitaries were then treated to a major, free nosh-up provided by the School Meals Service in the dining hall. This was also just that little bit more elaborate than your conventional pie, beans and chips. For staff to receive unlimited free food of quality in the dining hall at a time when even paid-for portions were decidedly parsimonious was like Christmas come early!

In fact it was around that time that I had begun to suspect that the portions of chips in particular were decidedly lighter than the advertised 4oz (or 113 grams). So one day I took a small plastic bag into the dining hall and slipped my served portion into it before running up to my room to weigh them on my chemical balance.

That then enabled me to pop back down to advise the Cook in Charge that my chips only weighed 86 grams, so the portion was about 25% light. Somehow I felt I never received quite such parsimonious portions of anything after that. Into the bargain, both the dining hall regime and the quality and healthiness of the menu have improved so much in recent years. In particular, we have come a long way from the constant call of "Chuuups!" from the front counter as yet another emptied tray needed to be replaced. Chips are one item which has almost disappeared from school dinner menus in the current health conscious age.

But let me return to important personages, and the day late in February 2001 when John Considine stopped me in the corridor. "Have you got a minute?" he asked as he somewhat furtively pointed towards his office. By now I had been the school's press officer for a few years and this was on a "need to know" basis.

The cover story for security purposes was that we were to be visited by a prominent member of the Scottish Executive. But (and this had to be kept confidential until his arrival) the real visitor was actually going to be Tony Blair. Clearly there was a major PR opportunity here. John of course wanted to make the most of it and wanted me to give him a willing hand.

At this point, pre-Iraq, Blair was at the peak of his popularity and less than three months short of comfortably winning a second term in the 2001 General Election. His visit to see this Scottish comprehensive school (and hence *"education, education, education"*) in action would be major news. I have always believed that Inverness Royal Academy was chosen for that visit as a prime example of a successful secondary school.

Inevitably the cover story didn't hold up for long and very soon, rumour – in the face of which I simply had to plead ignorance – was sweeping the place that it indeed was Blair who was coming. My status as school press officer meant I had to assist a large number of visiting media and gave me carte blanche to travel throughout the building with the entourage. As a result I witnessed every nuance at first hand.

Along with us was Sixth Year pupil Dawn Campbell who was official photographer for the day and she was able to get her memory cards off to Rena Fraser in computing quickly enough for the photos to be printed out for very willing Prime Ministerial signatures before his departure.

This was part of my description of the visit in that term's Newsletter. This time the headline was "YES PRIME MINISTER, IT WAS A GREAT DAY!" - which indeed it was.

"The task of welcome, after the Rector greeted him from his car, fell to the First Year who were lined up outside the building where a multitude of handshakes mingled with the cheers. Then it was into the front concourse to be introduced to members of the Pupil Council by Head Boy David MacDonald and Head Girl Fiona Cliff. There were more introductions in the Rector's office where invited guests - David Stewart MP, Highland Council Convener David Green, Education Chair Andy Anderson, Provost William Smith and Director of Education Bruce Robertson – awaited, and then it was off on tour to meet more pupils and staff."

Next up was a 25 minute session in Room 32 with senior History and Modern Studies pupils and it was at the end of this that the Rector came into his own and created what for me was the most memorable moment of a memorable visit. Proceedings were already running seriously late, so John dramatically broke into Blair's exposition on devolution, the Euro and his meeting with George W. Bush to declare: *"This is the only chance I'm ever likely to get to ask a Prime Minister to wind up but we're due in the library for video conferencing."*

Within seconds we were walking along the middle corridor towards the library and I suddenly became aware that here was John striding along with Tony Blair and, immediately behind them, here was I with none other than Alastair Campbell!

Tony Blair, who autographed several photographs that day, with Rector, Head Boy, Head Girl and class reps in the front concourse

There was little doubt in my mind even from that brief encounter as to who was really running the Blair show out in the public domain at least. However I can safely say that I was never nearly as prescriptive to John about what he needed to say in public as Campbell notoriously was to the PM!

Then there were various other formalities, including languages teacher Mary Grady singing "Viva Espana" to Mr Blair in Spanish, the signing of a multitude of autographs and a gathering with senior figures in John's office. With that all gone through, he then departed from the front door, but not before being ambushed by the media pack, including the BBC's Political Correspondent John Pienaar, demanding answers about the latest controversy surrounding Peter Mandelson.

The valedictory hand shaking ritual must have been wonderful preparation for his forthcoming election campaign. Our great anxiety here was that some of the junior school "worthies", parked out in the front drive, would just continue to behave themselves until he had fully and finally departed - which they did.

John Considine's reaction to the day, again quoted from that term's Newsletter, was upbeat in the extreme when he said: *"It was a* marvellous occasion for Inverness Royal Academy and a great success. The visit lasted twice as long as originally scheduled and the Prime Minister met many more pupils and staff than expected. He made particular reference to how courteous the pupils were and when he asked me why we were a successful school I put it down to staff commitment and also to a strong identification with the school by all involved in it."

It's a day which John still remembers well and it certainly was the highlight of my time as school press officer. More than a decade on, John told me: "I think it was actually Alastair Campbell who wanted to get a move on out of Room 32 so I just had to break in and off we went. I was especially impressed by the deference they all showed to the fact that although they were VIPs visiting the school, it was actually our place and we were in charge and organising it all. At one point David Green said to Blair, who had famously used the term himself very recently, that he was confident that he would find that Inverness Royal Academy was rather more than a 'bog standard comprehensive'".

I am sure he did!

Prince Edward's two visits were in 2003 and 2009. The second one was to meet participants in the Duke of Edinburgh's Award Scheme and we did like to think that this was in recognition of the school's huge involvement in it. This had been coordinated for many years by Pat Crippin of Modern Languages in conjunction with a huge number of other helpers and expedition supervisors.

This second visit mainly involved a gathering of pupils and staff from various schools in our library so Edward could see what was going on. But in the light of our previous encounter, there was one feature we didn't bother with.

During the 2003 visit, someone remembered the Blair experience and suggested that we should also get a signed photo of Prince Edward. I was asked to attend to the logistics so, within a much tighter timescale, I detailed my own daughter, who was in Fifth Year and a regular member of the school athletics team, to take the camera from our photographer at speed to Rena Fraser for uploading. Then Jenny had to bolt up the bottom corridor with the print as the Royal party was making its more ponderous way along the middle one back to the front door.

She made it with seconds to spare and handed the photo, just in time, to whoever was going to request the Royal signature – only for that poor individual, I forget who it was, to be told that Royals don't do signatures. So what a waste of time and effort that was.

Occasions such as the visits described do a lot to promote morale and a sense of identity within a place like a school. So, I have always felt, do any other opportunities for the institution to be seen in a positive light in the public domain. Internal morale is therefore one good reason for the institution to take steps to project itself publicly. But apart from that, it is equally important for the school to be seen publicly do be doing what it is doing well. The public, after all, pay their Council Tax in order for that to be achieved, so they need to be kept informed. So, even more importantly, do parents.

Duke of Edinburgh – Gold Award 1994

That is one of a number of reasons why I always thought that active steps in the area of public relations were always an important part of what the school should be doing.

Without a shadow of doubt, the Culduthel building does not have a fraction of the charisma that Midmills has. Royal Academy pupils of both eras will certainly retain affection for the institution – for the school itself. But it is unlikely that the Culduthel structure will be greatly missed by anyone when it is demolished on the opening of the new school – which prompts an interesting observation.

The Culduthel building of 1977 will be reduced to a pile of rubble after less than 40 years of life. Meanwhile Midmills, built from 1895, the school's original premises in Academy Street (1792) and Dunbar's Hospital on Church Street (1668), latterly home to the Royal Academy's predecessor the Grammar School – will all still be in active use.

There is probably an extra chasm between Midmills and Culduthel as homes of an Inverness educational tradition which stretches back to Dominican Friars in 1233. Not only was there a change of premises and of location out of the centre of Inverness. There was at the same time in the 70s a transition from selective to comprehensive education.

That was an amazingly complicated business which began with the Royal Academy not taking a first year in 1971 and only fully materialized into the 1980s, as described in the previous chapter.

In contrast, the move from Academy Street to Midmills in 1895 was merely a translation of half a mile of an institution which otherwise remained unchanged. Similarly the opening of the new building will involve only a physical shift of just a few yards. But in all these moves the school has taken with it many of its traditions, values and a lot else of great importance.

Now in 2013 I prepare to depart Inverness Royal Academy, 36 years after becoming a teacher there, 48 years after becoming a pupil and 56 years on from that JFK moment in Mrs Reid's front room back in 1957. And I trust that these traditions and values will be sustained undiminished as the school moves on.

7 - FULL CIRCLE

This series of Stephen's Brae books might never have seen the light of day but for how I happened to spend some evenings in the school's Bicentenary summer of 1992. The Queens Park running track was being upgraded so Inverness Harriers, courtesy of Millburn Academy which had inherited it, became temporary guests at the old Royal Academy field at Diriebught.

My return to the old field where I had spent so many happy hours of PE, rugby and athletics prompted me to feature it in an occasional series of articles I was doing at the time for the Inverness Courier. That 1992 effort was so well received that I then arranged to walk round the old school itself for the first time in 13 years to absorb inspiration for a more general follow up about school life at Inverness Royal Academy.

That visit to what had become Inverness College's Midmills campus was made within days but it was a year later, in the autumn of 1993, before the second piece finally appeared.

Just after I filed the copy, Maude died and since she figured prominently, I asked for a brief delay in publication. The article was then lost for a whole year before eventually surfacing from the bottom of a filing cabinet in the Courier office and suddenly appearing in the paper. This time the response was even more positive - so much so that it gave me the inspiration to write an entire book about my own secondary school memories. John Considine, when I approached him early in 1994, very readily agreed to this being published through the school, with profits to school funds.

By now I was deeply involved in coverage of the protracted merger which led to the formation of Inverness Caledonian Thistle FC so it was a further year before "Up Stephen's Brae" was ready. That in itself was a bonus since publication then took place on February 25th 1995 – the centenary of the opening of the very Midmills building which the book was written to celebrate.

"Further USB" and "Right USB" followed in 1999 and 2009 and now we have "Completely USB" which appears on my retiral from teaching after 36 years on the staff at Inverness Royal Academy.

So if this series of books originates from a walk round the old school in 1992, it seems fitting that it should also conclude with a similar expedition 20 years later. That is what this final chapter is all about - the valedictory walk I took round Midmills during the summer holidays of 2012.

Since that previous walk round, I had only once briefly crossed the threshold for Caledonian FC's final AGM, at the time of the formation of Caley Thistle in 1994. But it's not as if I hadn't passed the outside of the building often enough during the many intervening years. Midmills Road and Crown Circus for me have always been frequently used thoroughfares. Over these years it still took a while to get used to the retreat of the boundary wall towards the building in order to widen Midmills Road, a change which brought the new pavement just feet away from the Smokers' Union.

Inevitably, as Inverness College began to look at relocation to UHI's new campus at Beechwood, there could not have been much of a case for expensive maintenance of the building's exterior, which had deteriorated. But what I really wanted to see was the inside and a very helpful janitor gave carte blanche to go where I chose. I was also able to take photos which the College Estates Office has subsequently been good enough to allow me to use in this chapter as a record of how the place looks in 2012.

I decided to use my freedom of movement about the premises to enter by the one means which, in earlier days, had been more or less forbidden to pupils - the front door.

Immediately I walked through it, the first memory-evoking stimulus was the very one which had spontaneously overwhelmed me on my previous visit - the smell. Or perhaps I should say "smells" since they evolve and merge subtly in various parts of the building. They have barely changed at all in the near half century since I first became a pupil in 1965. So I found myself assailed once again by exactly the same odour in the front hallway as had instantly caught my notice on my previous return. The moment it impinged on my olfactory system, I once again spontaneously returned to these grand old days of the 60s, as pupil memories instantly flooded back.

The Midmills building has two main smells - more if you count hybrids of the originals. They can both simply be described as "foosty" and I will not even attempt to achieve any more detail than that through mere words. They are readily distinguished from each other and are clearly very persistent. The first inhabits the oldest parts of the building at the front and possibly has something to do with the parquet flooring which has very likely been there since 1895 and will have been lacquered repeatedly by successive janitors.

The second is a subtly different "foostiness" which is more a feature of the 1960 extension where the original and distinctive cream lino tiling with its repeating pattern of yellow rectangles, pictured on the next page, still covers the floors in the corridors in all its glory. There are not too many places in that building where some combination of these nostalgic odours doesn't still persist. Indeed, even as I type this on my computer at home, I still imagine I can sense these very nasal stimuli which, although "foosty" were vastly preferable to the frequently less pleasant aroma which wouls diffuse along the corridor from the dining hall.

Corridor separating the new building assembly hall and lab 21

Even in 1992 there had been substantial internal changes since my days as a pupil and teacher at Midmills. I was in no doubt that there would be more this time and indeed the building had once again evolved over these years. But strangely enough, the first change I spotted actually amounted to a return to an even earlier era which predated my own time at the school.

When I was a pupil, the first thing that greeted visitors as they walked through the front door was a cabinet packed with an impressive array of trophies, some of which now reside in a similar home in the front concourse at Culduthel. The actual cabinet is no longer there and the gap reveals a door which I never actually knew existed. Older FPs will remember it as the one through which D.J. MacDonald and his predecessors would have emerged into the old hall to take "prayers" first thing in the morning.

DJ taking assembly – or "prayers" - mid-1950's.

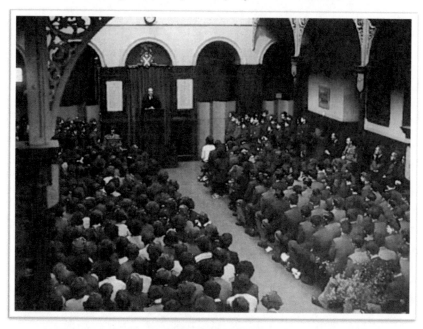

Same view in 2012.

When the 1960 extension, which included a new and much larger hall, was built, partitions were placed parallel to rooms 3 and 4 and to 5 and 6. These extended upwards to the base of the first floor gallery and round the far end where the grand staircase is. This created a smaller, self-contained area which became the library as well as corridors on which these four classrooms now were, and these corridors also had doors into the new library. The old door into the hall was then covered over with the trophy cabinet but is now exposed again in all its glory.

The ghost of Oddjob at lunch time, still roaring "Gerroutside!!", continued to waddle through that former library.

The classroom numbers changed somewhat after the refurbishment so the 3, 4, 5 and 6 I've just mentioned may not be completely familiar as such to an even earlier generation of FPs. Also changed forever are the functions of various rooms throughout the building and in some cases the rooms themselves have in whole or in part disappeared or had partitions added.

For instance the Rector's office near the front door, on whose royal blue carpet a goat from Balnafettack Farm was said to have defecated during an April Fool prank in the 70s, houses a Senior Lecturer in Business and Management.

For decades I have been totally at home with a completely different institution occupying my old school. But to me, this was still Willie Fatlips' personal territory, just as to those older and younger it will have been that of D.J., Ian Fraser or maybe even William Crampton Smith.

Similarly I wondered what Miss MacGill, who joined as an office junior in 1922 and retired in 1969, Mrs Stewart or Louise Munro would think about their adjoining secretaries' office now accommodating the Head of Faculty - Life Sciences and Creative Industries.

A circuit of the library corridor reminded me of the time in Third Year when we made the same trip chasing each other and were lucky not to be belted by David Thom. Then it was time to go up that majestic stairway which splits left and right from a wide landing en route to the upper gallery. It was on that landing, beneath the war memorial, that drama performances and concerts were given in the old, old days.

Even though the memorial has been at Culduthel since the late 70s, I still stopped for a moment half way up the main stairs where it used to be, thinking of the even chance in Normandy in 1944 when that farmhouse and its occupants became victims of friendly fire.

Then I moved on up the rest of the steps and on reaching the upper gallery, I found it carpeted! The only bit of carpet I remember in the entire school in my day was the stuff the goat later soiled in the Rector's office. I also found Curly's Room 16 locked - which in a strange sense was a fitting metaphor for the exclusivity which he exercised on the place, with no other member of staff to my recollection ever allowed to teach within its surrounds. Had I been able to gain access, I would have found it much changed since it now houses a computer suite and printing unit.

But had it still contained its four square array of lidded desks, I am prepared to believe all these decades later that they would - uniquely in the history of education - still have remained unblemished by human pen, pencil or biro. On the other hand something Leo Longmore told me did somewhat contradict this strong memory. When she moved next door from Room 15 to 16 on succeeding Curly as Principal Teacher in 1973, she says she remembers desks which were a lot less than pristine. Perhaps his standards slipped in his latter years, when I certainly found the former wartime secret agent a lot mellower than before.

Progressing along the first floor corridor immediately above the front door, I recalled the five different subjects taught in the sequence of rooms 7 to 11 - English (Fritz then Eddie Hutcheon), German (Miss Clark), French (Torquil), Gaelic (Lachie Dick and Duncan MacQuarrie) and Maths (Allan Wilson). It was impossible also not to acknowledge once again the absolutely vital part that the first and last of these played in my education. From Macbeth and Death of a Salesman to the sine rule and calculus, good English and Maths teaching were central to absolutely everything.

Main stairs - 1895 building.

Half way along that transverse thoroughfare I stopped and looked up. But there is now no sign at all of any conduit to the bell tower for the bell rope which at 8:55 and 1:55 each day would be tugged by Alec Munro or Oddjob or Jack McCall, causing those ascending Stephen's Brae rapidly to accelerate their gait for fear of detention for lateness from waiting prefects, whose powers are now long since diminished.

And I wonder if the Project Development Manager is aware that his or her office opposite Room 11 was in a previous era the Fifth Year boy prefects' room which also had something of a reputation as a safe house for amorous couples after school.

Inevitably in over 30 years of use by Inverness College there have been structural changes, and one of the most notable is the complete removal and even the walling up of the old cloakrooms. In particular the First and Second Year ones in the linking passage between the front part of the building and the Science, Art and PE block which was added in 1912 have all been walled up.

On leaving the former junior cloakroom area and having passed the coal cellar which became the Sixth Year common room, I did feel obliged to bite the bullet. So I held my breath and wandered into the boys' toilet across the corridor from the Prefects' Room at the old boys' door which first afforded me access to Inverness Royal Academy on August 24th 1965.

However, I need not have worried since one smell which does seem to have departed the place over the years is the frequently ghastly one which hung around these toilets. On the other hand a lot of the original fitments - urinal, hand basins and even the metal drinking fountain - are still there. There is one definite and significant change though. Back in the 60s you would NEVER have found a notice on the wall advising the practice of safe sex!

The other vile Royal Academy stink which used to haunt the place was the one which hung about the boys' gym. The odour of stale sweat is horrible indeed and in the old days it became immediately noticeable the instant you poked your nose into that gym. However, before embarking on that investigation, I did manage to confirm that the wooden cupboard which Robert Preece used to keep at the gym door, and which the Sixth Year boys used to turn upside down on a regular basis, is long gone.

Then to my delight it emerged that the old gym contains nothing more offensive than the kind of innocuous musty whiff which was perfectly consistent with it now being used as a sculpture studio. The adhesive marking tape for the badminton and basketball courts has been removed, but it was still perfectly possible to see the lighter coloured parallel strips on the floor indicating where these had once been.

Boys' Gym with the door to Bill's office at the far end.

Along similar lines, there were no gymnastic beams left, but the metal holes into which they were bolted were still there in the floor.

The old boys' gym is now part of the College's Art department. So also, across the corridor, is Room 17 where Pete Higgins gave me my first Chemistry lesson just over a decade before I too became the junior member of the department. Hairy Hugh's Room 18 no longer has a door but has become a photographic studio with a lowered ceiling, accessed from 17. On Room 17's outer wall in the corridor there still sits the same ancient radiator from which, in 1966, some miscreant managed to remove the cap and flooded the entire corridor.

The next stage of this expedition in educational archaeology involved close inspection of the Art Stairs bannister where the imprints could just be seen from the metal studs - now removed - which used to be inserted down its length to stop over exuberant pupils from sliding down it. Briefly I climbed the stairs to reacquaint myself with Music Rooms 23 and 24 where I spent much of my Sixth Year discussing the great classics with

Ian Bowman and Ruth Grant. Then on into the corridor comprising general classroom 25, to which Miss MacKenzie took register class 1A to check our details after assembly on that very first morning in 1965. Also the three art rooms - I could still almost hear Buckie's voice booming out from 26 - and Biology labs 29 and 30.

Art stairs.

However, the real shock came when I began to look for the Science Prep Room linking Labs 19 and 20. The latter was for a while the territory of Fred who used to cook his lunch over a bunsen burner in that prep room whilst glowering at classes working through Physics questions. The former was the Head of Chemistry's lab, and hence the preserve of Tomuck Fraser followed by Jim Sim and then Jim Dunlop.

The prep room is no more! It has been converted into a stairwell with fire exits and a completely new stairs running upwards to somewhere near Bobbuck Wright's Biology room.

From here it was only a few more steps to the 1960 extension. That originally comprised six classrooms, a huge assembly hall and stage and a dining room plus the Second Master's room, the men's staffroom and the medical room. At the time the whole lot cost just £114,000, albeit in an era when you could get good seats in the pictures for half a crown.

Instantly I made a beeline for the assembly hall because I wanted to relive the wonderful adventure which had been the Television Top of the Form quiz of 1970. I was completely taken aback to find the place in almost total darkness, since it has been converted into a drama studio. This also means that three of the largest plate glass windows in Inverness are now blocked off. How I had feared for the safety of these windows when I briefly went back to the school for that very last Caledonian FC AGM towards the end of the merger battle in 1994. Given how heated things had got at previous meetings in the Rose Street Hall, I expected the worst but by now things were quietening down.

The blacked out room did nothing to dim memories of so many experiences within that hall and in particular Top of the Form, which I relived whilst standing alone in the dark. At Eddie Hutcheon's insistence, I had captained that team whilst in Fifth Year although colleagues Irene Anderson, Margaret MacDonald and Andrew MacDonald were all in S6. We had finished runners up in the UK competition before winning the international series against the Dutch. The Owl Trophy, with which I am pictured on P153 both in 1970 and in 2013, still sits in the cabinet at Culduthel. The international series was pre-recorded at schools in the UK, including ours, and at the Dutch broadcasting centre at Hilversum, which until then meant nothing more to me than a name on a radio dial.

More to the point, we were unbeaten at home in both the domestic and international series. In the first, under the sweltering heat of the BBC's lights, we had seen off Leominster then Lymm right in the middle of my Highers before losing the final in Salisbury. Then against the Dutch during the summer holidays, victories back in that hall over Eindhoven and Deventer provided the cornerstone of the international success and ensured a home record of "played four, won four". Support from our schoolmates and from Inverness as a whole had been phenomenal and very influential in our success.

That whole international series had ended with a Great Britain v Netherlands international select match recorded at Hilversum where I had been fortunate enough to be a member of the GB team. Two of my three colleagues were from Salisbury and the remaining one from the third British school, Aberdeen Academy. Provost Smith's wife had even been good enough to travel out to Holland to support us.

I was highly amused at the time, and indeed somewhat motivated, by a number of the Dutch supporters having brooms with them which they were waving about in the air. This was a clear reference to the Dutch Admiral Maarten Tromp who, following a success during the Anglo-Dutch wars of the mid-17th century, is said to have lashed a broom to his masthead in a claim that he had swept Cromwell's navy from the seas. But there was to be no repeat because Team GB won the international handsomely.

As the distinctive Top of the Form theme music echoed back through my head, along with a reprise of the rapturous and inspiring applause of our support, the vision suddenly faded, then changed. Now it was time to revive other memories of that hall. There were drama productions such as Macbeth, School for Scandal and The Browning Version. There were operas too, like Carmen, Cosi fan Tutti and Dido and Aeneas which would then be succeeded later in the 70s by The Pirates of Penzance, The Gondoliers and The Little Sweep.

The hall was also where I had sat most of my "O" Grades and Highers before the Sixth Year Studies exams which were somewhat less ardently pursued after the unconditional for Edinburgh had been achieved. Once again the ghosts of Bill MacKell and Louise Robertson paraded between the desks which Bill Murray had meticulously set out, distributing papers before telling us we could start. Then, in that Macbeth-like procession of kings, it was their turn to be ousted by Alec Munro who, at assembly on that first day in First Year in 1965, we thought was the Rector!

In the corridor outside I could still see the patient dividing line of prefects separating queues of youth travelling in opposite directions towards their classes after assembly. Sometimes rather less respectful specimens from the junior years would aim anonymous, sly kicks in the passing at members of that thin blue and yellow line.

There are now flimsy tables and chairs in place of the stout benches whose occupants the equally stout Maude addressed from her blackboard in the nearby Room 21, whilst dishing out reams of notes on mechanical advantages and gold leaf electroscopes. Out in the back car park, Maude's space right beside the assembly hall door - into which she glided her Hillman Minx at precisely 30 seconds to nine each morning - has now been allocated to the disabled. Given how totally uncompromising she was about newcomers taking "her" chair in the ladies staff room, even the Disability Discrimination Act would surely have bowed in deference to Maude's possession of that space being nine points of the law.

Also still out in the car park are the huts which are now half a century old and really struggling as viable structures. My Higher and SYS Physics classes with Andrew Halkett then Jim Wilson had both been in hut 38. It was here also that we became aware of their identical trait spontaneously to scuttle into the cupboard when Maude was spotted waddling in their direction across the back car park.

Beside them in the car park is that cuboidal structure which was built in the early 70s to accommodate Biology, Business Studies and Technical, but which only contributed to the life of the school for a mere half dozen years.

I was delighted to discover that Room 22 had become a "rehearsal room". Because this means that the original tradition of entertainment still continues there - even though this is no longer in the form of Allan Beattie's hilarious monologues to squads of boys responding to the instruction "everyone round the front bench."

"Rhubarb and bananas! Wood doesn't grow on trees laddie!"

Meanwhile the adjoining space, where Mr. Beattie kept his "material", has now become a paper store.

The dining hall, where grace was religiously said before "meat, poodeen, ta'ees an' veg" were distributed, in that order of priority, strangely seemed smaller than I remembered it, but the old partition separating it from the hall is still there.

By this time, my morning coffee had had its diuretic effect so it was handy to be close to a familiar, albeit once again changed landmark. But as I relieved myself one more time in the Sixth Year boys' toilets, I realised that I was standing on the very spot where, at our last Christmas dance in December 1970, an over enthusiastic reveller had been obliged to kneel on the floor and vomit copiously into the bowl, simultaneously invoking the attentions of Hughie, Bert and Ralph. The identity of this individual, a former hostel boy who is a good friend, will remain undisclosed!

Above these toilets runs the short first floor corridor which housed Geography, History, Jimmy Johnstone's careers office and the balcony which overlooks the hall. Once again extra partitioning made the layout unfamiliar to the eye. Old echoes of Abdul's latest hissy fit at a miscreant still reverberated along from 34 towards 31.

All that was missing now from my tour was what had, in the 50s, metamorphosed from the Primary Department to the Girls' Wing. The Girls' Gym, originally the Primary assembly hall, has now reverted to type since it has become a play area for young children. Meanwhile the cookers are long gone from Miss Rose's Domestic Science room which, as a venue for "Oil Painting Studies", is little more than an empty shell.

The doors which gave way to the Girl Prefects' Room, and to a Ladies' Staffroom which used to be able to boast the greatest density of cigarette smoke in the Western world, are still there. So also is the one which used to say "Lady Superintendent". Once again I marvelled at the fact that this is the widest door in the building and recollected with a smile the theory that this originated from the time in the early 60s when Maude held that particular post.

This is the last of many mentions of dear Maude in this series of books. That frequency is very possibly a subconscious acknowledgement of her status as the first major influence I had from the realm of the physical sciences. This final reference is also appropriate given that the series was also inspired by a newspaper article which was delayed by a whole year when she died. She deserves a place among the giants of my educational experience at Inverness Royal Academy.

And with that, my tour was complete, provoking the strangest of schizophrenias where one part of me wanted to stay just a little longer but another was craving closure by departing.

I could have left from the door at the end of that girls' corridor. But even before I arrived I had evolved a different exit strategy.

Given that the main reason for any visits over the previous last 30 odd years had been for the purpose of researching books which were now complete, this would very likely be the very last of my very many departures from this building. Consequently it would have to be by that boys' door which had first afforded me access to Inverness Royal Academy almost half a century previously. It was through that very same door that I had left six, then 14 years later in my final acts as a pupil then as a teacher in the Midmills Building. This time I would be carrying no maroon duffel bag as in 1971 or box of chemical equipment as in 1979, but a simple notebook and camera.

The Quad – the forbidden route runs from right to left across this photograph.

Out of sheer devilment, I made my way back to my chosen exit via a diagonal sweep across the quad from the janitor's office to the interface between the Science block and the new building. This was the route, totally against traffic regulations, which we risked during a frantic rush from several classrooms at the front of the school to the dining hall in an attempt to get to the front of the queue and to favoured serving spoons. As in the 60s, I took just the quickest glance to my left into David Thom's office to ensure that my transgression had gone unobserved by the Depute Rector.

During that trip across the quad, which is relatively unchanged, I also had another of these "lottery fantasies" in which so many of us indulge from time to time. I thought that if I really hit it big on Euro Millions (which I don't actually do) I would buy the entire premises when the College was finished with them and give the place a really good upgrade. Then I would turn it into an Inverness Cultural Centre to accommodate a museum, library, arts centre and office accommodation for voluntary organisations and sports clubs.

Relocating the museum would also enable me to dip further into my nine figure winnings to fund the demolition and replacement of the Bridge Street monstrosity which in the mid-60s came to blight the city centre on the demolition of the fine old buildings I had passed during that walk up to Mrs Reid's.

Hence I finally emerged from the boys' door into the small car park where Bill Murray left his Ford Anglia and Hairy Hugh his Morris Oxford and where we had bodily carried Lesley Anderson's Fiat 500 right into the angle of the building outside Room 3. By now the fantasy had evaporated and reality had reasserted itself.

That regrettable reality is that, as I write, no one knows exactly what will happen to what is a still fine building. As this book goes to print, an understanding seems to be emerging that the College will vacate the premises early in 2014. It has a proud past and thoroughly deserves a distinguished future for many decades to come.

Then what overwhelmed me was the thought that, barring the unforeseen, I would probably never set foot in the place again.

Inverness Royal Academy's Midmills building provided me with a six year educational experience which was highly fulfilling and, in certain ways, life changing. It also gave me a chance to teach there for a year and in 2011, I became the last Royal Academy teacher still in post to have taught regular classes within its walls.

It also provided the inspiration and subject matter for this series of books which now also reaches its conclusion. It would have been impossible for an adult, never mind a four year old, to have conceived the prolonged impact of the institution which first made itself known to me through Mrs Reid's front window that afternoon in 1957. But now the time has come in most respects to let go.

The schooldays concluded decades ago. So did the year when I was privileged to teach there. The fourth and final book about it all now also reaches its conclusion. The "Stephen's Brae" series is certainly on the short list of things in my life of which I am most proud. And as I write, my 36 years on the staff of Inverness Royal Academy are now also all but over, as the school contemplates moving into its fourth different premises in just over 220 years of history. Culduthel, with its leaking roofs and

1970s "sick building" pallor will never have the same charisma as Midmills. However, buildings are mere fabric. As one gives way to another, the overwhelming thought has to be that what matters is the institution - and that continues to move on with distinction through time.

The boys' door, a conduit for many memorable entrances and exits.

Labore et Virtute